Edwin Pinder Barrow

Regni Evangelium

A Survey of the Teaching of Jesus Christ

Edwin Pinder Barrow

Regni Evangelium
A Survey of the Teaching of Jesus Christ

ISBN/EAN: 9783337166786

Printed in Europe, USA, Canada, Australia, Japan

Cover: Foto ©Lupo / pixelio.de

More available books at **www.hansebooks.com**

Regni Evangelium.

A SURVEY OF THE TEACHING OF JESUS CHRIST.

BY

EDWIN PINDER BARROW, M.A.

WILLIAMS AND NORGATE,

14, HENRIETTA STREET, COVENT GARDEN, LONDON;
AND 20, SOUTH FREDERICK STREET, EDINBURGH.

1892.

SALISBURY:

BENNETT BROTHERS, PRINTERS,

JOURNAL OFFICE.

PREFACE.

Sooner or later there comes to every thoughtful student of the Christian religion a twofold desire. First, to search for the true image of "the man Christ Jesus" under the false colouring of sacred art. The figure familiar to us in picture and poem is not, we know at last, the real form of Jesus of Nazareth, of the work-shop and of the fishing-boat, provincial in habit and dress and speech, stamped with the marks of a roaming life, hardened by rough usage, scorched by wind and sun, stained with road-side dust, or wet with mountain dew.[1] In a ruder age, no doubt, the soft

---

[1] It will be said of course by some that Christian art is conventional and symbolic, that its object is to present the spiritual and not the historical aspects of things, and that for this reason it shrinks from realistic reproduction. There would be more weight in this objection if Christian art, with Christian hymnody, had always kept to the early symbolic images of the Passion and had never descended to the coarse realism of later representations of the Crucifixion. If realistic treatment is permitted here, why not in other scenes of Gospel history? But we venture to go further and to say that the temper of the present age—an age in which religious emotion is but little excited by the images of art—values, as antiquity did not, fidelity to fact, and finds both moral incentive and spiritual elevation in the endeavour to realise the plain realities of a life really loved because really human. It is the hard literalism of the Evangelist, rather than the softened symbolism of the artist, which has driven the story of that earthly life deep into the hearts of men.

A 2

imaginings of Christian art were not without use to
teach a gentler life; but it is time, we feel, that all
conventionally false, though tender, delineation should
cease, if in the portraiture of Christ there is to be left
one touch of his masculine strength. And, indeed, the
facts of his life are majestic enough without being
idealised. There is more to move men's hearts in the
rough image of the living Christ "travelling in the
greatness of his strength," than in the softly pictured
scenes of his helplessness and woe. We are of those
who "would see Jesus" as they saw him who knew
him best. The circling halo, the rich robes, the soft
colouring, the delicate outline, the outward grace, the
hints of inner mystery—these were unknown to the
men who saw and heard and looked upon and handled
the Word of Life. But these true reverence needed
not then. Does it need them now?

The second desire is a longing to find the actual
gospel of the great Teacher under the false rendering
of sacred science. A gospel was conceived, was preached,
was believed, was counted sufficient for salvation, in
which the birth and the death of Christ held no place.[1]

[1] The intimations of impending suffering and death—Matt.
xvi. 21. Mark viii. 31. Luke ix. 22. Matt. xvii. 12, 22. Mark
ix. 12, 31. Luke ix. 44. Matt. xx. 18, 22. Mark x. 33, 38.
Luke xviii. 31—are no part of Christ's public teaching, and are
in all cases said to have been given to the disciples privately.
Against this clear and united testimony, the veiled announce-
ments reported to have been made to 'the Jews' and to 'the
multitude' in John viii. 28; xii. 32, can hardly be allowed to
weigh.

It was "the gospel of the kingdom." Can this gospel be recovered?

Modern criticism is doing something every day to encourage and to satisfy this double desire. The critic once sat amidst the ruins of buried religions and tried from scattered hints to depict the unknown. The past was reconstructed in the light of the latest theory. The problems of thought, as of language, were solved by ingenious conjectures. But the day of speculative fancy is over, and the age of exploration has begun. The student works now with pick and spade. He takes his own corner in the field and does his best. His business is not to reconstruct, but to lay bare. His learning need not be very profound, but he must have a quick eye and a patient, honest hand. The result of his labour will never be anything more than a contribution, and its value cannot be known until the whole has been examined and arranged. And, as in the ruined heaps of Chaldean cities the unearthed tablets give the inscriptions of earlier and of later periods of religious belief in one disordered mass, so in early Christian literature we have to deal with a body of fragmentary records, once of certain date and authorship, but now strangely thrown and heaped together; of great historical worth, though in many parts without historical sequence. But, as the tablets now in our museums have rewarded the research of scholars by falling into chronological order and by revealing the development of creed out of creed, so, under the patient handling of modern inquirers, not only the separate writings of the New Testament, but the separate portions of those writings, have in some measure been reduced to a right series both in time and in value. Putting it broadly, there are four stages in the history of early Christian teaching ; first, the period of oral utterance by Christ himself in his own country and in his own tongue ; then the period of oral narration by his friends and followers at various centres in translated form ; then the period of free literary compilation, in a highly literary language, of current spoken narratives ; and, lastly, the period of still freer literary comment on these written summaries, with the use of ecclesiastical and philosophic terms. Evidence of each of these stages may be discovered in unequal proportions in each of the Four Gospels, and out of these successive layers of matter thrown into one confused aggregate we have to separate the contributions of the first speaker, of the reporter, of the compiler, of the commentator. The result and the reward will be a clearer view of the person, action and character of Christ, and a closer grasp upon the essential and permanent elements in his religion. For, indeed, Christianity is not a religion of the Person of Christ addressed to him, but his own personal religion reproduced in us. Not what we think and feel about him, but what he thought and felt about God and human life—that is the essence of the Christian faith, and the practice of it is the test. Not without pain and loss, at first, do we reach this position ; but to some men peace comes easily through authority, and to others tardily by inquiry ; and to some the only revelation is a bygone outward flash, and to others it shines also in the inward growing light. It is difficult to unsay the creed of early years, impossible, perhaps, to remould the worship of a life-time, but certainly hopeless to attempt to force the mind always to be content with those first half-reasoned judgments which were formed before the whole evidence was heard, before the argument was rightly understood.

" Whatsoever is not read in Holy Scripture, nor may be proved thereby, is not to be required of any man, that it should be believed as an article of the Faith." There is indeed a sense in which the Bible is an " impregnable rock ;" but to quarry into Scripture to repair the foundations of Faith, is to find many a stone which honest builders must refuse.

*** Passages quoted from the Old and New Testaments are given in the words of the Revised Versions throughout.

ERRATA.—P. 60, Note i. For Luke xxv. 34, xxvi. 29, read Matt.
xxv. 34, xxvi. 29.
P. 107, Note i.   For Ezra xxi. 21, read Ezekiel
xxi. 21.

CONTENTS.

" Laws penned with the utmost care and exactness, and in the vulgar language, are often perverted to wrong meanings ; then why should we wonder that the Bible is so ?"—*Swift*.

" Scripture, like other books, has one meaning, which is to be gathered from itself, without reference to the adaptations of Fathers or Divines."—*Jowett*.

" Experience proves surely that the Bible does not answer a purpose for which it was never intended. It may be accidentally the means of the conversion of individuals ; but a book, after all, cannot make a stand against the wild living intellect of man, and in this day it begins to testify, as regards its own structure and contents, to the power of that universal solvent, which is so successfully acting upon religious establishments."
—*Newman*.

CHAPTER I.

Jesus of Nazareth.

I. MANNER OF LIFE.

THE 'Life of Christ' begins for us, as it begins in history, with his ministry. Feeling our way through a shadowy mist of poetry forced into prophecy and fulfilled in legend, we touch the first solid fact when we read that "Jesus went about in all Galilee, preaching the gospel of the kingdom."

A low flat-roofed cabin, entered and lighted by one door ; the floor strewn with rushes ; a ledge jutting from the wall and serving as a seat or a shelf by day, a bed by night—such, probably, was the home of Jesus at Nazareth. A table no higher than a stool, with mats for seats, this was its furniture. Leathern bottles hung from the roof, a mill and a meal-tub and a bushel-measure were on the floor. Sometimes the measure was turned up on end to serve as a stand for a lamp. To find a piece of money dropped in that dark, straw-littered room, the lamp must be lighted and the floor must be swept. Homely objects and homely actions these, but dear to him because of early days and for ever sacred to us because of their after use.

B

"And ye shall teach them your children." It was from his parents that Jesus received his first teaching. Portions of the Law in Hebrew and passages from the Psalms and the Prophets were his first lesson-books. At the age of five he had begun to know them by heart. Elementary synagogue-schools were not, perhaps, generally established until afterwards, but Jesus as a child may have received some such further instruction. "How knoweth this man letters having never learned?" meant only that he had not passed through the lecture-room of any Rabbi. That he could write we have no certain knowledge. Aramaic, the vernacular of Palestine, a corrupted form of Hebrew, was the dialect of his home and gave form to his thoughts; Greek he would hear and learn to speak out of doors, for it was the only common language of a mixed population; of Latin, the language of the Italian garrisons and settlements, he would know little; whilst the literature of either Greece or Rome would be a forbidden and impossible study.[1]

[1] At the same time some acquaintance with Greek and Roman thought would not be difficult. Heathen traffic from Decapolis to the coast and from Eastern and Western Galilee to Central Palestine crossed and recrossed the plains below the hills of Nazareth. Sepphoris, "the pride of Galilee," and Tiberias soon to be its capital, with their mixed populations, and Capernaum, with its Roman garrison and custom-house, were within easy reach. The Lake of Gennesareth was fringed with Italian villas. The priests and worshippers of idolatrous temples formed part of every crowd. It is usual to speak of Nazareth as a "quiet and secluded village" and to apply to Galilee of that day the language of Isaiah's time. At the date of which we are speaking Nazareth, if not itself a station on a Roman road, was

" Seest thou a man diligent in his business ? he shall stand before kings." Thus the Wise Man taught the dignity of toil. It was part of the sturdy morality of the Jews that every boy should learn a trade. The greatest of the Rabbis followed the humblest callings. Teachers who held it to be a reproach to take a fee from a pupil did not disdain the wages of manual labour. Jesus was known to his countrymen as a carpenter and the son of a carpenter. No occupation could better combine discipline with freedom. Whilst it trained hand and eye, it left both body and mind uncramped ; it could be pursued at home or abroad ; there was in it neither that coarseness of out-door toil which makes thought impossible, nor that pettiness of sedentary work which often makes thought unhealthy. There was no lack of holidays in the Jewish year. The fifty-two sabbaths and the fifty-nine feast-days educated and refreshed the Jewish workman.

surrounded by a dense and busy population, and was probably more civilised and more enlightened, though less strictly Jewish, than many of the towns in the South. Peter and John, natives of Galilee, though easily perceived to be " ignorant and unlearned men," (Acts iv. 13) were able, if tradition is to be trusted, not only to speak Greek, but also to write in that language. It has even been contended that Christ habitually spoke Greek ; Roberts, *Greek the Language of Christ and His Apostles* ; but, on the other hand, see Neubauer, *Studia Biblica*, 1885. On the question whether Peter and James could have written the exceptionally good Greek of their Epistles without the scholarly aid of an interpreter, see Simcox, *The Writers of the New Testament*, p. 68, and Salmon, *Introduction to the New Testament*, pp. 508, 546.

A long white, or striped, tunic of linen girded by a sash; over this a blue cloak; on his head a white kerchief falling behind and fastened with a cord in front; his bare feet shod with sandals—this was the dress of Jesus. Pharisee and Scribe and Sadducee, courtly Herodian, Greek merchant and Roman soldier had each his distinctive robe or uniform. In the streets of Jerusalem it was not possible to confound the higher with the lower orders. To the lowest order Jesus was content to belong. Addressed by some as Rabbi, hailed by others as a king, revered by a few as the Messiah, he still retained to the last the dress of a poor Galilæan workman. It is said that he " became poor;" more worthy of remembrance is the fact that he remained poor.

His food was of the simplest—bread and fruit and fish and honey.

As for money, no one ever owned so little. Whatever he earned at his trade he seems to have given to the support of others. Afterwards, as a teacher, he was dependent on a thirteenth share in a common, but ill-filled purse. A sudden demand for so trifling a sum as the temple-tax he was unable to meet. They might gamble for his clothes at the foot of the cross; there was nothing else to divide.

Of one rich possession no one could rob him—bodily health. We read of long marches by day, of long watches by night, of exposure to heat and cold and storm, of rest and sleep hastily snatched, of unwearying attention to the demands of . others, of work done under the strong pressure of excited crowds, or undertaken at a moment's notice in answer to a distant call. Not that his life was without pain, but it was the pain of over-strained strength, not of sickliness incapable of effort.

II. Characteristics.

There is no figure in history so detached, so independently personal, as that of Jesus in the Gospels. Reject what you please in the written narrative, and there still remains a personality intensely real, salient, distinct. Happily this narrative is not a complete biography by one contemporary hand. The biographer is wont to project too much of himself into that on which he works. But in a collection of recollections repeated from mouth to mouth, though much may by play of imagination be distorted and confused, yet much also by force of repetition will be isolated and preserved. The hero's words and actions are largely at the mercy of each narrator, but his original central individuality is left comparatively untouched. Regard in this light the work of the Evangelists. They are compilers, not authors. They begin without preface, they relate without comment, they end without a moral. The action of the drama—for drama it is—is stately and even. There are no asides, no artificial emphasis, no elaborated climax. There is only enough of detail to make persons and places distinct; the central figure is therefore never obscured. Their interest in their subject is extreme, they may be themselves a part of that which they present, but in presenting it they are unimpassioned, impersonal. It is their very artlessness which produces an effect beyond the sweep of the highest art, and the absence of all effort to create an impression goes far to produce it.

It will not be difficult, then, to note the leading lines of that strong character which for eighteen centuries has thrown a spell upon mankind.

1. First we may mark the sensitiveness to the outer world of nature, a quality, as has been well observed, singularly absent in S. Paul. To Jesus earth was the far off echo, the answering flash, of heaven. Two worlds were his, and, more than any before him, he discerned the hidden laws which rule them both. Sky and sea and air are searched by his observant eye. The reddening cloud, the trackless wind, the corn sprouting in the furrows, tangled with weeds, choked by thorns, whitening to harvest; the birds following the sower, building among the branches, gathering their young under their wings, falling dead to the ground; the field-flowers careless of their life and unconscious of their beauty, the mustard-tree and the fig-tree in the hedge— all these touch him from without and are touched by him with new meaning from within. It is to the " desert-place "—some cool, unfrequented spot—the " mountain " and the " garden" that he betakes himself

for rest or for prayer. The occupations of men are also a thoughtful study; the labour of the fishing-boat, of the vineyard, of the market, of shepherd and plough-man and merchant and steward; the building of a house or of a tower; the giving of a feast, the welcome of a bridegroom, even the games of children.

2. He is accessible and sympathetic. The great teachers of the world have not always stooped to the world; have often avoided it. But he throws himself into the social life of the day, declines no interviews, refuses no invitations. He is equally at the call of patronising Pharisee, Roman officer, and wayside beggar. He is welcomed at a banquet, and at the bedside of the sick. Timid women bless him—bless even the womb that bare him—and children are not afraid to be taken to his arms.

3. Of his fearlessness there are many instances. On the same day, when all hearts fail, he faces the madness of the waves at sea and the madness of the hunted demoniac on the shore. "Herod will kill thee;" "The Jews of late sought to stone thee;" are warnings which have no weight. Single-handed he seems to have made an attempt to clear the temple-precincts of an unholy traffic. Plots thicken round him and he alone is calm; each thrust is met and turned aside; and at the close of his life he is undismayed by the swords and torches of his pursuers, the cries of his accusers, the threats of his judges, the barbarities of the guard-room, the taunts of the mob, the pains and terrors of the scourging-pillar

and of the cross. For fifteen hours he endures and flinches not a moment.

4. Closely joined to courage is the power of self-control; for half the secret of strength is restraint in its use. He who was not afraid to face his enemies is not afraid to disappoint his friends. Conscious of power he can still arrest it at any point. They would make him a king, but he can nowhere be found, and, in an hour of still greater excitement, a crowd carries him in triumph, but he allows it to disperse. Self-restraint with a motive may be called prudence, but his was not the prudence of selfish caution. He would not give occasion to the authorities for a charge against himself, but still less would he be the cause of harm to loyal followers. "Are ye come out as against a robber?" is an assertion that his power with the people had never run into violence.

Another form of self-control is the subdual of impatience. The apathy of some, the prejudice of others, the interference of his friends, the slow apprehension of his disciples must often have tried him sorely. But they draw no retort, no petulant remonstrance, only questions of surprise; and the last unfaithfulness of Peter is chided only with a look.

5. Prompt and resolute in action and direction, asserting his claims as a leader without hesitation, he is at the same time unexacting in the demands which he makes for himself personally. A few simple commissions to buy bread or to prepare a lodging, and one

request to watch with him in prayer, are all that we read. There is no insistence upon outward homage, no urging of his own needs, no complaint of neglect, above all no teasing tests and trials of affection.

6. Decision of character does not exclude gentleness. The firmness of Christ was balanced by a readiness to reason and to be reasoned with. " Learn of me for I am mild and lowly of heart." The words may or may not have been actually used by him of himself, but that the qualities had been recognised is clear from S. Paul's appeal to the Corinthian converts " by the mildness and sweet reasonableness of Christ."

7. But the most marked, perhaps, of all his personal characteristics is his reverence. By " reverence" we do not mean only a certain attitude towards certain objects, places and times. We mean that in the inmost heart of all things he saw something to be revered. He was not sanctimonious, but no one ever felt so deeply the sacredness of life. Kind and engaging, and not without sense of humour, there is no room in his mind for levity, and still less for mockery. He exposes, but never jeers; there are touches here and there of satire, but not of ridicule. To him every-thing was solemn because everything was of God. This solemnity he felt in prayer and worship, but also in the mysteries of nature; if he discerned it in the Scriptures and in temple-ritual, he saw it no less in all the relations and ministries of men and in the innocence of children in their midst.

If we dwell on his characteristics as a teacher, we may note :—

1. First, the absence of mystery. The word is spoken "as they were able to hear it," but he has no esoteric doctrine. He can say with the Buddha that "his hand was not the closed fist of the teacher who keeps some things back."

2. Nor is there any appeal to rigid authority. "Verily I say unto you" is a constant form of introduction. By an intuitive sense he fastens upon truth and presents it because it is truth and not because it has been pronounced to be true. Therefore he teaches, to the astonishment of the people, with authority, and not by authority, as the Scribes.

3. He is sanguine and hopeful. Compare the figures of the prophets and their burdens of woe with his attitude of promise and encouragement. Nor is it the vague hopefulness of those fond restorers of fallen liberties "qui ont pris les souvenirs pour les espérances," who colour the future with the glories of the past. He draws no false picture of an impossible Israel. Rather does he dispel their dearest national hopes and abates not a little of his own for his people. But the thought of a brighter day runs through all his words.

4. Nor is he ever too profound for his hearers. Not in language. The meaning of his words, it is true, is often missed. That even his disciples had grasped but little of the spirit of their master's teaching, is painfully evident in the history of the Apostolic Church. But

his speech is always transparent. His vocabulary is that of daily use, his illustrations are those of daily life. There is no setting forth of abstract terms with further abstractions to define them. Everything is concrete and familiar. Now and then a paradox is thrown in to excite attention, but there is no studied wrapping up of thought in philosophic phrase.

5. Further, he deals with nothing outside the bounds of his own conviction and experience. There is no throwing out of questions for debate, no discussion of problems from which the speaker is remote, no tasting of intellectual joy in free and novel speculation. A practical turn is always given to speculative inquiry.[1] He teaches, not a system of religious thought, but a life, a life which he has lived and deems to be within the reach of all.

6. His method is sober and serene. There are no devices for catching, or for holding, attention. He never feels his way, or lowers his theme, or his tone, never qualifies or excuses or retracts. Class-interests and class-prejudices are not played upon; opinion he neither flatters nor defies. He informs, he soothes, he inspires; he talks to men of their wrong, not of their wrongs; but he shows no eagerness to hasten or to test the effect, or to reckon his hearers. He appeals to the moderate spiritual affections of which all are conscious and capable, rather than to the rapturous sensibilities which may be excited in a few. He does not measure

[1] Luke xiii. 23, 24, &c.

his work by success or by failure, but by 'to-day' and ' to-morrow.' The one does not elate, the other grieves, but does not mortify. He does not seek the crowd or wait for the crowd to seek him. He opens his mind, as he goes, to many or to few, but, this done, he leaves them, and the result, and passes on. His attitude is not that of the professor in his school, nor of the philosopher in the grove. He is the pilgrim-teacher; more earnest than either; more humble, yet more independent; more gracious, yet more dignified.

7. And his crowning distinction as a teacher is this, that his ministry was a ministry of contact. He touched men into discipleship. He recognised no line of sepa-ration, social or religious. It was defilement to come near the leper, he touched him; it was defilement to be touched by a fallen woman, she might kiss him; it was degradation even to be in the company of publicans, he ate with them. Had he simply preached, like John the Baptist, the common people would have heard him gladly—for a time. The prophet's strength as a prophet is his weakness as a leader. The points which mark his strong personality mark also the limits of his personal influence. John came neither eating nor drinking and he was therefore never at home, never in close touch, with his hearers. His attitude was open to two constructions, so that, whilst some mused in their hearts whether he were Messiah himself, others said bluntly that he had a devil. But this new priest of humanity, though not like the Baptist of priestly

line, called nothing common or unclean. It is said that he took our nature upon him and so exalted it. The phrase by itself carries little meaning, or, if meaning, little comfort. Rather we may say that our nature rose to its full height in him and that only from that high point would he view it in others. In an unintended sense it was truly said of him that he knew what was in man—he knew what man has it in himself to be. This hopeful gaze through eyes abashed into the buried life within worked wonders. It revealed men to themselves. To find fault is easy; to find it is very often to fix it; to overlook it is to leave it very much where it was; but to look over it, looking for and expecting something else—this is sometimes to touch the spring of a new life. This was the Great Teacher's secret. As much by his belief in them as by his love for them he drew men unto him.

8. To look once more, before we pass from this subject, over the whole field of Christ's religious teaching, is to be struck by its breadth and openness, its directness and its fairness, the freedom which it asserts and the freedom which it allows. It stands apart from the teaching of the Schools which gloried in minute application, in fine distinction, was full of petty casuistry, had spun the ancient law into an infinity of novel regulations, had made religion unspiritual and was fast making it unpopular. The contrast will show itself more clearly in the next section of this chapter.

III. The Teaching of the Day.

A strong ethical vein runs through Judaism in all its stages of development. Conduct, it has been said, may be reckoned as three-fourths of human life. Right conduct, or righteousness, might almost be reckoned as three-fourths of the Old Testament. " Ye shall be holy : for I the Lord your God am holy ;" " Offer the sacrifices of righteousness ;" " To him that ordereth his conversation aright will I shew the salvation of God ;" " In the way of righteousness is life ;" " What doth the Lord require of thee, but to do justly, and to love mercy, and to walk humbly ?"—these are but a few of the many passages which, in general terms, emphasise the fact that without morality there can be no religion.

And the general principle is applied in every form of particular regulation. The claims of the poor and the stranger, of the fatherless and the widow, even of the lower animals ; the duties of the married state, of parents and children, of proprietors and employers, of lenders and borrowers—all are considered, set down and proclaimed. If only this ethical system had been allowed free course and had been rightly followed, there would have been little in Jewish morality for even Christ to reform.

But side by side with the rule of right conduct ran the rule of ritual, or right worship. How to walk with even step between these two lines has always been the .

problem of religion. For most men have a bias to the ceremonial, rather than the moral, side. Religion on the side of worship engages the affections, gives definite consecration to certain times, places and objects, is fixed and precise in its demands, and secures for its votaries open and ample recognition ; but religion on the side of rectitude, or right dealing, rather controls than indulges the emotions, calls nothing common or profane, leaves many of its claims to the conscience of its followers, and rewards them often only with their own virtue. That the people of Israel were inclined from time to time to prefer the exact performance of outward rites to the more difficult discharge of moral obligations, is shewn again and again by the appeals of their prophets. " To obey is better than sacrifice," is the protest of Samuel. " To what purpose is the multitude of your sacrifices ?" " Bring no more vain oblations ;" " Your new moons and your appointed feasts my soul hateth ;" " When ye make many prayers, I will not hear ;" " Cease to do evil : learn to do well"— this is the remonstrance of Isaiah. " Trust ye not in lying words, saying, The Temple of the Lord," is Jeremiah's last reproof just when the temple itself was about to fall and the sacred ark, the holy fire, and the oracles on the breast of the high priest were on the point of being removed, never to be restored. Only a violent overthrow and a long exile would teach such blinded worshippers that religion may spread itself gloriously towards heaven, and yet be dying at the root.

But, after the Return, there arose by degrees a misleading influence even stronger than that of priestly ordinance. To an over-elaborated ritual succeeded an over-developed doctrine. "The priest was overtaken by the jurist." The Law of Justice and Mercy and Love was now too simple for a refining age. The common rules of life were, in the eyes of the learned, "beggarly elements." The whole duty of man, once written on the heart, bound between the eyes, talked of in the house and by the way, the familiar legend of private door-post and common gate-way, must henceforth be a complicated code whose interpretation shall be the secret of a School. The last prophet had spoken, the priest stood indeed by the nation's one altar, but the 'lawyer' was abroad. Of accumulated tradition, impenetrable because unwritten, he alone had the key. He only could decide how a sacrifice should be offered, or how a feast-day should be kept, but he was even more careful to determine how a bath should be filled, or how a platter should be cleansed. Under his guiding hand, the hand of a blind leader of the blind, the people lost all insight into their own Scripture ; the quickening spirit was killed by the paralysing letter ; intellectual activity was of more account than moral effort ; the study of precept was made more honourable and more attainable than its practice ; and the ancient Law, majestic in its simplicity, was again broken, and broken by the hands of its custodians, into the thousand useless fragments of a petty and vexatious legalism.

At the same time there was one tendency of Jewish thought which, though affected by time and circumstance, was never at the mercy of any caste or school. This was what is termed the Messianic Expectation— the common heritage of all—the hope of One, the Anointed of Jehovah, who would revive a glorious past and bring in a yet more glorious future. The golden age of the Jews, as has often been said, lay even more in the time to come than in the days that were gone. But as this central hope, with their own history, rose or fell, so did the figure on which it was centred shrink or expand. A king of the house of David, a heavenly being, a prophet, a mighty warrior—these were the various shapes imaged in various minds under various moods. An oppressed nation contracts in time its own ideal, and under Roman rule the people of Palestine would have been well content if a nameless, unconscious Messiah, found in the desert or in the secret chamber, had come forth unattended to lead them in open revolt. How far the popular conception had fallen from the vision of the prophets and of the earlier apocalyptic writers may be gathered from many chance words interwoven with the Gospel narrative. Scarcely has the Baptist begun to preach, when all men reason in their hearts concerning him whether haply he be the Christ.[1] It may be, Lo here! or, Lo there![2] for no one knoweth whence he cometh.[3] Peasants and fishermen may aspire to be his officers.[4] A simple mother

[1] Luke iii. 15. [2] Luke xvii. 21. [3] John vii. 27. [4] Mark x. 35.

c

dreams of the highest posts of honour for her two sons.[1]
His subjects shall eat at his table,[2] and drink new wine
with him,[3] in his kingdom. A quarrel between two
brothers is not thought too small a matter for his
attention.[4] Can this be the Christ ? asks a woman who
declares that in a few minutes she has heard all that
ever she did.[5] A similar instance of apparently miraculous knowledge forces the same conclusion upon a
Galilæan disciple.[6] If he would give proof of his title,
let him only command that a stone become bread, or
cast himself down from the gable of a temple-cloister.[7]
The servants of the high priest will be satisfied if,
blindfolded, he will prophesy ;[8] the chief priests and
scribes, if he will come down from the cross ;[9] the
rulers, if he will save himself.[10] The highest flight of
national hope is that he may redeem Israel,[11] and by
redemption is meant no more than the restoration of
the kingdom.[12]

This, then, is the lower Messianic hope expressed
in the language of the day, but the thought of a later
generation reverts to the more exalted type. Angels
of God ascend and descend upon the Son of man ;[13]
he sits on a throne of glory to judge the twelve tribes
of Israel ;[14] and in the minds of some he even comes

---

[1] Matt. xx. 21.   [2] Luke xxii. 30.   [3] Matt. xxvi. 29.
[4] Luke xii. 13.   [5] John iv. 29.   [6] John i. 49.   [7] Luke iv. 3, 9.
[8] Matt. xxvi. 68.   [9] Mark xv. 32.   [10] Luke xxiii. 35.
[11] Luke xxiv. 21.   [12] Acts i. 6.   [13] John i. 51.
[14] Matt. xix. 28.

on the clouds of heaven, attended by angels, and before him are gathered all the nations of the world.[1] The non-fulfilment in Jesus of certain Messianic signs leads to a second conception, that of a second advent. Disappointment brightens into hope deferred. To that day are postponed the terrors and portents, famines and earthquakes, wars and plagues, apostasies and persecutions which are the true birth-pangs[2] of the Son of man. The predictions of the First and Third Gospels are the prophecies of Isaiah, Ezekiel, Joel, Amos and Daniel re-written and renewed.[3]

We may now grasp something of the field which opened before the eyes of Jesus of Nazareth—a people still inclined to righteousness, though its first meaning had been forgotten ; attached to the ritual of their fathers, but less under the touch of a priesthood now declining in power and remote from daily life ; fiercely devoted to the Rabbinical law which preserved the unity and distinctness of their race, and yet groaning under its burdens too grievous to be borne.[4] How should such a people be approached ? How could religion like this be purified and lightened ?

Note.—It is difficult to say with certainty whether the Jews before Christ regarded Messiah as simply human, or as a pre-existent being of a higher order.

---

[1] Matt. xxvi. 64. xxv. 31, 32. Cf. Daniel vii. 13.
[2] 'Ωδῖνες, Matt. xxiv. 8. [3] Cf. Matt. xxiv. 6—31, Luke xxi. 8—28, and marginal references *ad locc.*
[4] Matt. xxiii. 4. John vii. 19. Acts xv. 10.

Originally they seem to have expected, not an individual
Messiah, but a dynasty of kings of the house of David.
In this unbroken theocracy Christ would "abide for
ever" (εἰς τὸν αἰῶνα; cf. 1 Macc. xiv. 41). Subse-
quently the Messiah was thought of as a human king
and ruler, but specially endowed by God with gifts and
powers. See *Psalter of Solomon* xvii. 23, 41, 42, 46,
47. To some, on the other hand, though a created
being, he is pre-existent and superhuman. See the
Book of Henoch xlvi. 1, 2, xlviii. 3, 6, lxii. 7; the
Fourth Book of Ezra, xii. 32, xiii. 24, 52; and perhaps
Micah v. 2.—Schürer, *Geschichte des Judischen Volkes*,
Part II. Vol. ii. § 29.—The higher developments were
probably the result of the dogmatizing labours of the
Scribes, but that the lower conception was the more
popular in the time of Christ is clearly proved by such
passages as John i. 20—25, Luke iii. 15, Matt. xxiv.
24, Mark xi. 9, by the places in which Jesus is addressed
as the Son of David,—Matt. ix. 27, xii. 23, xv. 22, xx.
30, 31, xxi. 9, 15, cf. Rom. i. 3,—and by the care with
which the so-called Genealogies were drawn up to prove
his Davidic descent.[1] Ewald has shown very strikingly,
(*Geschichte des Volkes Israel*), how the more thoughtful
Jews, after a long series of disappointments, would in a
manner transfer to heaven the object of their undespairing
hope; confident that he would descend from thence

---

[1] Καὶ γὰρ πάντες ἡμεῖς τὸν Χριστὸν ἄνθρωπον ἐξ ἀνθρώπων προσδοκῶμεν
γενήσεσθαι, are words which are often quoted from Justin, *Dial.
c. Tryph.* 48.

when the moment for fulfilment had arrived. This divergence in the current conceptions of Messiah helps to explain the difference between the popular Christology of the Synoptic Gospels and the loftier contemplations of the Epistles. See 2 Cor. v. 16.

The bright image of King Messiah in Isaiah vii.—xi. is cherished and revived by Jeremiah and Ezekiel in the promise of a second David, even after the kings of Judah and Jerusalem had ceased to reign, but it dies away in the darker colouring of Jehovah's Suffering Servant in Deutero-Isaiah, xl.—lxvi. It is this change in the Messianic ideal that compels even Delitzsch to admit that these later chapters must be by a later hand.

The following references give, perhaps, the leading Messianic passages in the Old Testament which may be combined into a picture of the Ideal Kingdom, or King :—2 Sam. vii. 16, cf. 2 Sam. xxiii. 5; Ps. ii. 7, 8, 9, cf. Acts iv. 25, 26, xiii. 33, Rom. i. 4, Heb. i. 5; Ps. xlv., lxxii., lxxxix., cxxxii. 10—13; Isaiah ix. 6, xi. 1—10, xlii. 1—7, xlix. 1—6; Jeremiah xxiii. 5, xxxiii. 15; Ezekiel xxxiv. 23, 24, xxxvii. 24; Daniel vii. 14; Hosea iii. 5; Micah iv. 1—4, v. 2; Zechariah vi. 13, ix. 9, 10. Messiah, as the Ideal Prophet, is thought to be foreshadowed in Deut. xviii. 15, 18, and, as the Son of God, in Ps. ii. 7.

For the Messianic Prophecies in Historical Succession, see the work of Delitzsch under that title, Eng. Tr. 1891, and the two treatises on Messianic Prophecy by Riehm and Briggs.

IV. Titles and Functions.

Of the many current appellations of the expected Messiah,[1] the Christ, the Anointed, the following appear in the Four Gospels :—

1. *Son of David.* This title is given to Jesus by two blind men in Galilee ;[2] by a Canaanitish woman ;[3] by a blind man, or two blind men, at Jericho ;[4] and by the Passover pilgrims.[5] It is also stated by the Scribes and Pharisees to be one of the Messianic names.[6] But the view that the Messiah must necessarily be born of the house of David is corrected by Jesus himself.[7]

2. *King.* This title, implied in the first, is found under different forms. To the disciples generally Jesus is The King that cometh in the name of the Lord ;[8] Nathanael addresses him as King of Israel ;[9] it is part of his accusation before Pilate that he claimed to be An anointed King ;[10] the chief priests and Scribes ask in derision that The King of Israel should come down from the cross ;[11] and the super-scription of the cross is The King of the Jews.[12] The title in this last form Jesus accepts,[13] but neither by this nor by the first (Son of David) does he ever describe himself.

---

[1] The title in its Hebrew form, Græcised, occurs only in John i. 42, iv. 25. The term Christ in its Greek form is never used in the Gospels as a proper name, but always as an official title.
[2] Matt. ix. 27.   [3] Matt. xv. 22.   [4] Matt. xx. 30.   Mark x. 47.
[5] Matt. xxi. 9.   [6] Matt. xxii. 42.   John vii. 42.
[7] Mark xii. 35—37. [8] Luke xix. 38. [9] John i. 49. [10] Luke xxiii. 2.
[11] Mark. xv. 32.   [12] Matt. xxvii. 37.   [13] Matt. xxvii. 11.

3. *He that cometh.* Art thou he that cometh ? is the question put by the two disciples sent by John the Baptist.[1]

4. *The Holy One of God.* In the synagogue at Capernaum a man with an unclean spirit declares that by this name Jesus is known to him.[2]

5. *The Chosen of God.* · Scoffingly used by the rulers at the Crucifixion.[3]

6. *Prophet.* This term also is variously applied. Sometimes Jesus is to the people definitely The Prophet,[4] or The Prophet that cometh into the world ;[5] but oftener he is A Prophet,[6] or A great Prophet,[7] and even by his disciples after his death he is described only as A Prophet mighty in deed and word before God.[8] The title is not rejected, for he hints that as a prophet he is unacceptable in his own country,[9] and declares that as a prophet he must not perish out of Jerusalem.[10]

7. *Son of God.* In the Synoptic Gospels Jesus is addressed as Son of God by certain possessed with devils,[11] by the Twelve,[12] by Simon Peter ;[13] and in the Fourth Gospel by Nathanael[14] and by Martha ;[15] he is acknowledged under this title by a Roman centurion,[16] and by a man born blind.[17] In the First Gospel the

---

[1] Luke vii. 19. [2] Mark i. 24. Cf. John vi. 69, R.V.
[3] Luke xxiii. 35. [4] Matt. xxi. 11. John vii. 40. [5] John vi. 14.
[6] Matt. xxi. 46. Mark vi. 15. [7] Luke vii. 16. [8] Luke xxiv. 19.
[9] Luke iv. 24. [10] Luke xiii. 33.
[11] Matt. viii. 29. Cf. Luke iv. 41. viii. 28. Mark iii. 11.
[12] Matt. xiv. 33. [13] Matt. xvi. 16. [14] John i. 49. [15] John xi. 27.
[16] Matt. xxvii. 54. [17] John ix. 38.

title, on two occasions, is not refused,[1] and in the Fourth
Gospel is expressly claimed.[2] But its significance is
easily ascertained if we remember that it is one of the
official designations of the Messiah ;[3] that, so far from
being thought to have any peculiar, supreme, or preternatural, ontological sense, it is omitted altogether in
the three parallel passages which give Peter's famous
confession, and, in Nathanael's similar avowal, is fol-
by an equivalent title which would otherwise be a
strange anti-climax ;[4] that when Jesus is adjured by the
high priest to say whether he is the Son of God, he
shows by a simple assent that he has no wish to correct
the sense which was attached to the term in the mind
of the questioner ; and, lastly, that, if he in so many
words claims the title, he is careful also to explain that
he thereby says no more of himself than the Scriptures
said of others ' unto whom the word of God came'.[5] It
is a title to which any member of the Kingdom may
aspire.[6] In the Synoptic Gospels the later metaphysical
meaning of the expression never appears, except, perhaps,

[1] Matt, xvi. 16. xxvi. 64. [2] John v. 25. ix. 35. x. 36. xi. 4.

[3] It is true that the term does not appear in earlier Jewish
literature as one of the Messianic titles, but its use by the high
priest would seem to imply its recognition as a name for Messiah.
It was probably derived from Ps. ii. 7, a passage which was certainly applied to Messiah by Jewish teachers. Cf. John i. 34.
xx. 31.

[4] 'King of Israel,' John i. 49. [5] John x. 35.

[6] Matt. v. 9. Luke xx. 33. Cf. vi. 35. If these Evangelists
had ever attached any awful, superhuman, Trinitarian meaning
to the title Son of God, would they not have hesitated to apply
the same words to members of the Kingdom ?

to a certain extent in Matt. xi. 27 (Luke x. 22) and Mark xiii. 32. But see Appendix III.

Beside these Messianic names there is the title *Son of man.* This designation (not reckoning the parallel passages) occurs in more than fifty places in the Four Gospels. In itself it carries no fixed meaning. It may be applied with propriety to any one who in any sense is typical of his race.[1] To lead the hopes of men, or to share their pains, or to understand their thoughts, is to be a son of man. If the term was really adopted by Jesus, if it was his habitual self-chosen appellation, if it was free from previous association and from all remoter meaning, then, by a familiar Hebrew idiom, it indicated to those who heard it an avowal of closest kinship with everything essentially human. At the same time it carried with it its own limitation.

Orthodox commentators, almost without exception, consider the title ' Son of man ' to be one of the Messianic names because of the similar expression in Dan. vii. 13, (B.C. 167—165 ?), and they support this view by extracts from the Book of Henoch (B.C. 130 ?) in which the same expression is undoubtedly applied to Messiah. But the prophet in his vision sees one ' like unto a son of man,' *i.e.*, in human form, and thereby distinct from the four ' beasts ' which were typical of

---

[1] " The True Man, the Single Normal Representative of realised Manhood," is Godet's explanation ; but that is to think into the term more than a Jew could gather from its use in his own Scriptures.

four successive earthly empires, and this human form is to him symbolical of that holy people in which God's holy kingdom would ultimately be advanced ;[1] and in the apocryphal vision also the object is still ' a son of man,' a created, if not a human, being. "There is nothing," says Dr. Westcott, "to shew that the title was (popularly) understood to be a title of Messiah ; " and, again, "It is inconceivable that the Lord should have adopted a title which was popularly held to be synonymous with that of the Messiah, while he care-fully avoided the title of Messiah itself." In the same way it has been argued by Réville and others that there would have been nothing novel or spontaneous in Peter's confession (Matt. xvi. 16) if his Master had already claimed and used a Messianic title. Dr. Liddon contends, indeed, that the question put to the disciples —' Who do men say that the Son of man is'—was meant to draw more than a confession of Messiahship, that the question was really, What is the Messiah, "in the seat and root of His Being ?" and that the answer is given in Peter's words, "The Son of the Living God." If this be so, it is a little singular that this answer should be altogether omitted in the parallel passages (Mark viii. 29, Luke ix. 20, John vi. 69). But, to re-turn, "There is nothing," says the Bishop of Durham, " to shew that the title was understood to be a title of Messiah." "It was to Jewish ears a clear assertion of Messiahship, a constant setting forth of his Messianic

[1] See vii. 27. Cf. 18, 22 and ii. 44.

dignity," says the Bampton Lecturer. When authorities so eminent are at variance, it is difficult for others to speak with any confidence, but there is reason for thinking that it is doubtful whether Jesus ever really described himself officially, or even personally, by this name. That in preaching the Kingdom he used the prophet's term in the prophet's sense is probable enough, but, if he applied it to himself individually, how are we to explain those passages in which, in the very front of his ministry, ' the Son of man' is made to claim almost more than Messianic dignity and power?[1] If he " carefully avoided the title of Messiah itself," are we to believe that he boldly advanced these astounding pretensions in the presence of hostile witnesses who neither challenged them at the time nor brought them under the notice of the Sanhedrin afterwards, when they would have furnished most convincing evidence against their prisoner at his trial? An examination of the passages in which the title under discussion occurs will show that they bear, almost without exception, on the Christ's supreme prerogatives and on his return in glory and with power from heaven, and we may conclude that, whatever meaning may have attached to the first use of the term amongst the first disciples, it was soon lost in the eagerness with which later followers read into the title ' the Son of man' all that was predicated of ' a son of man' in the above-mentioned prophetic and apocryphal visions.

[1] Mark ii. 10, 28. viii. 38. Matt. xiii. 41.

The passages named must therefore be received with caution.[1]

The reader has, perhaps, anticipated a difficulty which must here be noted. In the Synoptic Gospels Jesus enjoins secrecy as to his Messiahship,[2] but in the Fourth Gospel the title is openly asserted,[3] or accepted,[4] without any such injunction. And yet so wary an exponent as Bishop Westcott does not hesitate to say that, "From the circumstances of our Lord's examination before the Sanhedrin it is evident that He had not openly proclaimed Himself as the Messiah, or the adjuration of the High Priest would have been unnecessary (Matt. xxvi. 63)." Solve this as we may, we may still safely conclude that in the Messianic office Jesus did discern a means for guiding his people to their good. For nothing could equal it in its power of appeal. It appealed to a hope which, if narrow, was popular, passionate and pure. Faith in the future was to the Jew of that day a liberating force waiting only for the touch of a liberating hand. Faith in your own destiny is, in the history of reform, a motive as powerful as it is rare. In the reformer it is personal,

---

[1] After reaching this conclusion independently, the present writer found much of the argument ably stated and more fully illustrated in Carpenter's *First Three Gospels*, 1890. He was thus enabled to recast one or two clauses in the above paragraph. Otherwise it stands as it was written.

[2] Matt. xvi. 20. xvii. 9. Mark viii. 30. Luke ix. 21, 22.

[3] John iii. 13. iv. 26. v. 18. vi. 27. x. 25. xi. 27.

[4] John i. 41, 45, 49. vii. 26. viii. 24. ix. 22.

in the people national. When both motives are at
work, and come into contact, the energy evolved is
immense. Such energy did Jesus exhibit and evoke.
Confident in himself, he taught others to trust him
and to trust themselves. Knowing the purity of his
own aim, he did not hesitate to charge himself with the
guidance of an ambition which he could not wholly
approve, or wholly gratify. If the popular conception
of the Messiah had been dwarfed by foreign oppression,
there was still no name which held so powerful a spell.
Stronger than that of Priest or of Rabbi would be the
influence of the Anointed. And if under this name he
approached the people, first announcing and then
assuming the office, half-accepting and half-claiming
the title, he would be able to correct their mistaken
ideal. It is impossible not to see that when he says
that he came not to be ministered unto, but to
minister;[1] that he was in the midst of them as he that
serveth;[2] that he must suffer many things and be
rejected;[3] that his kingdom is not of this world;[4] that
he could be followed only by those who denied themselves;[5] that he was no judge or divider over self-
seeking rivals[6]—he is really correcting the small hero-
worship to which the nation's hope had shrunk. The
material he spiritualizes; that which is personal he
diverts; that which is local he extends.

The Christ must speak with authority. It is the

[1] Matt. xx. 28. [2] Luke xxii. 27. [3] Luke ix. 22. [4] John xviii. 36.
[5] Mark viii. 34. [6] Luke xii. 14.

first condition of his office. Hence the decisive ' I say unto you,' though Moses himself be over-ruled ;[1] hence the sharp 'Follow me,' though the living be thereby divided,[2] and the dead left unburied.[3] He reviews and revises, challenges and condemns. The priest is rebuked in his own precincts,[4] the teacher is denounced in his own school.[5] Once assured of his sincerity, there is no quality in a leader which men more admire than an unhesitating claim to an unreserved submission. He is not born to rule, if he argue, or justify, or explain. This imperious urgency is one of the proofs, as it is one of the secrets, of power.

The ruler disobeyed becomes a judge. The word that he has spoken, the same shall judge in the last day.[6]

On two occasions he pronounces forgiveness of sin.[7] In neither case does he claim independent power. In the former instance he is represented as saying that he had authority[8] to forgive sins on earth; and this authority he is stated to have transmitted to others.[9]

To this extent, then, does Jesus adopt and adapt the titles and the functions of the Christ. He is a prophet, a teacher, a liberator, a master, a judge; he is, in a

---

[1] Matt. v. 22, &c.   [2] Luke ix. 62.   [3] Luke ix. 60.   [4] Matt: xxi. 13.
[5] Matt. xxiii. 3.   [6] John xii. 48.   [7] Matt. ix. 2.   Luke vii. 48.
[8] 'Εξουσίαν, Matt. ix. 6, 8.   Mark ii. 10.   Luke v. 24.
[9] Matt. xvi. 19. xviii. 18.   John xx. 23.   And yet in heaven he is not the Forgiver of sin, but the Pleader with God for sinful man. 1 John ii. 1. Rom. viii. 34. 1 Tim. ii. 5. Heb. vii. 25, ix. 24.

sense, a king, and, in a deeper and more cherished sense, a Son of God. An impatient loyalty seats him afterwards on the clouds of heaven, the graves open at his voice,[1] and the nations are parted before him.[2] Who more worthy than he to wield these powers ? But did he really claim them ? Let the answer come from his own disciples who, if they had ever heard these claims, had strangely forgotten them. "We hoped," they say —and the sigh marks the range and the limit of their hope—" we hoped that it was he which should redeem Israel."[3]

To these preconceptions of the Messiah Jesus adds one new condition. The Christ must be prepared to die an early and violent death. So only could the new religion and the old be brought face to face and the trial of strength come to a final issue. There was no room in Jewish thought for a suffering, still less for a martyred, Messiah.[4] "We have heard out of the law that the Christ abideth for ever."[5] No wonder is it if Peter took him and began to rebuke him,[6] if the rest perceived not the things that were said,[7] if they were

---

[1] John v. 28.   [2] Matt. xxv. 32.   [3] Luke xxiv. 21.

[4] It is now generally admitted that there was no ante-Christian doctrine of a suffering Messiah. Isaiah's afflicted servant of God (ch. liii.) personifies the afflictions of God's people in captivity and exile. See Schürer, *Geschichte des Judischen Volkes*, Part ii. § 29, and, for the Jewish interpretations of Isaiah lii. 13— liii. 12, consult Hengstenberg, *Christology of the Old Testament*, vol. ii. 310—319, and the more recent work by Driver and Neubauer.

[5] John xii. 34.   [6] Matt. xvi. 22.   [7] Luke xviii. 34.

exceeding sorry.[1] But this added condition of readiness to die gives a different complexion to Christ's
assumption of the office of Messiah. He grasps at
nothing in embracing death. He personates no one, if
the part which he plays is cast by himself. For indeed
he was as far from fulfilling the prophetic vision as
from satisfying the popular expectation. Suffering and
death belonged as little to the divine ideal of David and
Isaiah as to the debased conception of the Herodian
age. The spiritual redemption of man was a project
beyond the flight of the Messianic dream, whilst the
death of the redeemer was a point to which it could
never have descended. Therefore, if Jesus assumed
the Messianic office, he also detached himself from
every Messianic theory. This, unfortunately, was never
understood. His followers, believing that Jesus was
the Christ, believed also that everything predicated of
Messiah must be predicated of him. Therefore in
presenting his character they decorate it with every
Messianic attribute. Before long the attributes themselves suggest modes of action, and modes of action
suggest particular events, and thus the life of Christ in
the Gospels comes to be written largely out of the
' prophecies' of the Old Testament.

We have spoken of Christ's purposed death. But
that purpose must not be misunderstood. Death was
to him a necessary crisis. He never speaks of it as an
atoning sacrifice, as a sacrifice at all. Beyond the bare

[1] Matt. xvii. 23.

announcement of the fact, there is nothing; of the propitiatory or expiatory effect, not a word. He is indeed reported to have said that the Son of man came to give his life a 'ransom'[1] for many (ἀντὶ πολλῶν, as in xvii. 27, without the sense of substitution). But

[1] Matt. xx. 28. λύτρον is that which looses and, as the context in no way helps to fix the meaning of the word, no strict forensic or sacrificial sense of 'ransom' ought to be forced into it. The former is excluded by the fact that a ransom carries with it the idea of compensation and is paid for deliverance from a foreign and oppressive power, and to that power. Origen was logically right when he argued that the 'ransom' of Christ's death could only have been paid to the Evil One. The sacrificial meaning of the word can be supported only by its use in Exod. xxx. 12, where the ransom could be paid, and was paid, by the ransomed, and not necessarily by another on his behalf. The analogy of the *kopher* cannot therefore be fairly pressed. In the New Testament the words connected with λύτρον (λυτροῦσθαι, λύτρωσις, ἀπολύτρωσις &c.) are so variously applied that neither of the above significations can be said to be determined by them. The notion of 'ransom' runs into the idea of 'purchase' in 1 Cor. vi. 20, Rev. v. 9, xiv. 3, and the thought in either form is more at home here than in its solitary position in the teaching of Jesus. The passage as it stands in the First Gospel has far more the appearance of a comment than of an original saying, and its oblique introduction under cover of the title " Son of man" is not, as we have seen, (p. 27) in favour of the latter view. Wendt (*Inhalt der Lehre Jesu*) thinks that the " deliverance from bondage" indicated is best explained by Matt. xi. 28—30. Cf. Deut. vii. 8, in the LXX. and Luke i. 68, xxiv. 21. But all discussion of the proper force of a special term like λύτρον seems to be idle, if it is itself only a translation of an unknown original expression in another tongue. ['Purchase-money' seems to be the meaning which Bp. Westcott attaches to the word in a Dissertation on the use of λύτρον which did not come under the writer's eye until the above note had been written. *Ep. to the Hebrews*, p. 295.]

D

so might any martyr to a sacred cause speak of himself,
looking to the results of his self-devotion. It is true
also that at the Last Supper he is said to have spoken
of his blood of the new covenant shed for many unto
remission of sins.[1] But the New Covenant was an
accepted phrase and carried a meaning already defined.
Jeremiah had written of the "new covenant" which
God would make ; "I will put my law in their inward
parts, and in their heart will I write it . . . . . for I
will forgive their iniquity, and their sin will I remember
no more" (xxxi. 31—34). It has been contended that
there is no mention here of a mediating sacrifice; that it
is rather by the exclusion of sacrifice that the covenant
is "new" and "not according to the covenant made with
their fathers."[2] But, without pressing this point, it is
sufficient to observe the fact that in the first age of the
Church the sacrificial aspect of Christ's death could
not present itself to those who had not yet broken with
Judaism. That " a great company of the priests were

[1] Matt. xxvi. 28. Mark xiv. 24. The same effect is ascribed,
however, in the same words, to the preaching of the Baptist in
Mark i. 4. In the earliest account of the Eucharist, 1 Cor. xi. 25,
the words of institution are given as, "This cup is the new
covenant in my blood." The difference in the doctrinal significance of blood shed in expiation of sin, and blood shed in
ratification of a treaty, is extreme. See Exod. xxiv. 8. On the
double use of διαθήκη as ' covenant' and ' testament,' see Westcott,
Ep. to Hebrews, 298.

[2] In xxxiii. 11, the idea of *eucharistic* sacrifice is certainly
retained. For the spirituality of the New Covenant, see Hosea
vi. 6, Amos v. 21, Micah vi. 6—8, and cf. Matt. ix. 13, xii. 7 ;
Hebrews ix. 10.

obedient to the faith,"[1] that the disciples " day by day, continued stedfastly with one accord in the temple,"[2] is decisive proof that in their minds at least the value of the daily sacrifice remained undisturbed. When afterwards the sacrifice of the altar was impossible to the Jew and forbidden to the Gentile, then " the sacrifice of the death of Christ" supplied a common want in the religions of both." [3]

It has been said that, if Christ did not perform miracles, he at least professed to do so.[4] To this it may be answered that, if he professed to work miracles, he at least minimised their value. " There shall arise false Christs who shall show great signs and wonders ;"[5] " Many will say unto me in that day, Lord, Lord, did we not by thy name do many mighty works ? ;"[6] " An evil and adulterous generation seeketh after a sign ;"[7] " He sighed deeply in his spirit, and saith, Why doth this generation seek a sign ? ;"[8] " By the prince of the devils casteth he out devils."[9] If Christ and his countrymen can thus speak of miracles, what becomes of their

[1] Acts vi. 7.

[2] Acts ii. 46. Cf. ii. 1, iii. 1, v. 42, x. 9, 14, 28, 30, xiii. 2, 3, xv. 5, xvi. 3, xviii. 18, 21, xx. 6, 16, 24, xxi. 20, 23, 24, 39, xxii. 3, 12, Rom. xiv. 5, Gal. iv. 10, v. 2, Col. ii. 16, Phil. iii. 2, Rev. ii. 9, iii. 9. vii. 5, xi. 19, xii. 1, xxi. 12, and see Lightfoot, *Galatians*, Dissertation III.

[3] The writer of the Epistle to the Hebrews, for instance, weans his readers from the consolations of the Temple, partly by presenting the Messiah as the eternal high priest who had offered one sacrifice once for all.

[4] *Ecce Homo*, ch. v.   [5] Matt. xxiv. 24.   [6] Matt vii. 22.
[7] Matt. xii. 39.   [8] Mark viii. 12.   [9] Matt. ix. 34.

D 2

evidential force? It is clear that in that day they were held to be neither necessarily divine in their origin, nor necessarily conclusive in their testimony.[1]

But the Gospel miracles, it is said, "are more than credentials, they are symbolical representations of redemptive action."[2] And here again the answer is easy. What serviceable connection can there be between redemptive action and an act which is not itself redemptive ? To cure physical blindness is one act, to remove spiritual darkness is another. The two acts are on different planes. The latter only is redemptive. That I can perform the first, is no proof that I am either willing or able to perform the second.

We may even go further and say that in founding a new religion the use of miracle would be immoral. The object in view is to establish a moral ascendency, to incite to moral endeavour. But the first effect of a miracle would be repellent and discouraging ; it would excite wonder and alarm ending in recoil. There might afterwards be recovery in the direction of gratitude, but there would be no moral appeal, no moral quickening. It has often been remarked that in the ancient world there was no necessary connection in men's minds between supernatural power and goodness.[3] If there

---

[1] Justin (*First Apology*) thinks that, without the argument from prophecy, miracles would not of themselves be sufficient to establish the divinity of Christ. In another place, " curing cripples from their birth," he says, "is little more than what you say of your Æsculapius."   [2] Liddon, *Bampton Lecture* IV.

[3] Pagan miracles were admitted by Christians, but attributed to demons.

was no necessary connection, there could have been in miracle no attestation to goodness, and therefore no incitement. " A moral power," says Professor Mozley, speaking of the Jewish exorcists, " a moral power might dismiss the demon that brooded on the understanding, as it does the demon that tempts to sin." It is in this field that we look for the miracles of Christ. In certain cases of mental and nervous disorder his " moral power" threw his patients under a strong enchantment. Evoking effort, he aroused energy. There was a moral challenge and a moral response, with secondary physical effects. In this way " virtue" went out of him, as it goes out still from those who have calmness of reason and purity of soul. Even now there is magical force in human look and voice and touch. But everything outside this area ascribed to Christ we may confidently reject. To play upon men's minds by playing upon water and loaves of bread, fig-trees, fish and swine—to do this he must be false to himself and to his aims. If he had possessed such power, he would have disdained its use. His own words, " Why even of yourselves judge ye not what is right ?" exalt the use of conscience and reason above dependence on outward signs.[1]

---

[1] There is a fine passage in the First Volume of Harnack's *Dogmengeschichte* which would suffer by translation and is therefore given as it stands :—" Dass er mit sich selber konnte, wie er wollte, dass er ein Neues schuf, ohne das Alte zu stürzen, dass er die Menschen fur *sich* gewann, indem er von seinem *Vater* kündete, dass er ohne Schwärmerei begeisterte, ohne Politik ein

Note:—Dr. Mozley, a strong defender of the Gospel miracles, ruthlessly exposes the argument of those writers "who urge that in a miracle there is no *violation* or *suspension* of the laws of nature, which go on but are *neutralised* or *counteracted* by a higher law." In the preface to the third edition of his *Bampton Lectures* he shows that, if the antecedent is new and strange, not the ordinary and constant antecedent, if it is an unknown power not in nature, then the phenomenon is not a natural fact at all in the scientific sense. Any such attempt, therefore, to reconcile miracles with the laws of nature in no way meets the objections, or satisfies the claims, of physical science.

He would have dealt in the same way, we imagine, with the 'höheres natürliches' of German apologists.

V. Dates and Records.

The Writer of the Third Gospel, in his preface, shews us exactly how the present Gospels came to be written. He is one, he says, of many who tried to draw up in connected narrative the common *tradition* respecting certain facts which had come down *from those who had been eye-witnesses* of the same. The day of personal testimony was, therefore, over.[1]

Reich aufrichtete, ohne Askese von der Welt befreite, ohne Theologie ein Lehrer war, immitten einer Zeit der Schwärmerei und Politik, der Askese und Theologie, das ist das grosse Wunder seiner Person."

[1] Cf. Weizsäcker, *Das Apostolische Zeitalter*, p. 381.

This traditional basis, whether oral, or written, or partly oral and partly written, is the common material used by the compilers of the three Synoptic Gospels.

From Acts i. 22 (cf. John xv. 27) it would seem that this primitive Gospel went no further back in the life of Christ than the "baptism of John." The original Gospel, therefore, finds its closest and most faithful rendering in the Second Synoptic Gospel, is further developed in the Third Gospel, and finds, perhaps, its latest expression in the First Gospel.[2] There is a close agreement between these three Gospels in form, substance and language. Where they recite the words of others, they are most in harmony; when they narrate events, they exhibit slight peculiarities of style.

Who were these compilers? It is impossible to say. Their works are anonymous and there is, therefore, no personal evidence. In the way of historical evidence, we find that Justin Martyr (d. A.D. 164) speaks of

[2] Evidence in favour of the priority of the Third Gospel to the First may, to the writer's mind, be found by a careful comparison of the following passages thrown into tabular form. Those from the First Gospel show an advance, sometimes in spiritual thought, sometimes in historical development, upon those of the Third. But the whole question of the order of the Gospels is beset by difficulty, for each may in turn be shown to possess fragments of "the gospel of the Kingdom" in its earliest form, and yet all exhibit marks of the influence of later ecclesiastical teaching and usage. Keim, in his *Geschichte Jesu von Nazara*, places the Synoptic Gospels in the following chronological order :—Matthew, A.D. 66; Luke, A.D. 90; Mark, A.D. 100. It is not meant, however, that each existed at the date affixed in its present completed form. Mark is placed last by Clement of

certain "Memoirs composed by the apostles and their
followers," and that Eusebius (d. A.D.340) has preserved
a few loosely-worded fragments from writings of the
second century to the effect that "Matthew, the apostle,
composed (or caused to be composed, συνεγράψατο)
in Aramaic 'The Utterances' [of Christ] ;" that "Mark,
having become Peter's interpreter, wrote down from
him, though not in chronological order, all that he could
remember of the words and actions of Christ ;" that
" Luke, the follower of Paul, set down in a book the
Gospel preached by Paul."[1]

Let us allow that the " Memoirs by the apostles
and their followers" is another name for the *Utterances* of
Matthew, the *Reminiscences* of Mark, and the *Summary*[2]

Alexandria, and with these authorities agree Baur, Schwegler,
De Wette and Köstlin. The majority of critics, however, would
place him first.

Luke v. 31, 32, compared with Matt. ix. 12, 13.
     „   vi. 3—5   „   „   „   xii. 3—8.
     „   vi.   „   „   „   v.—vii.
     „   ix. 20   „   „   „   xvi. 17, 18.
     „   xi. 2—4   „   „   „   vi. 13.
     „   xi. 29, 32   „   „   „   xii. 29, 32.
     „   xi. 39, 52   „   „   „   xxiii.
     „   xviii. 29   „   „   „   xix. 28.
     „   xx. 17, 18   „   „   „   xxi. 42—44.

[1] As S. Paul in his speeches and letters makes no reference to
the early years, discourses, or miracles of Christ, his Gospel, as a
summary of the Gospel narrative, would probably be brief indeed.
References to recorded sayings appear in 1 Cor. vii. 10, ix. 14,
xi. 23 ; 1 Thess. iv. 15—17. For an interesting note on the difference between the λόγοι τοῦ Κυρίου of Clement of Rome and the
λόγια of Papias, see Weizsäcker, *D. A. Z.* p. 387.

[2] 'Digestum' is Tertullian's word for the Third Gospel.

of Luke. But are we, therefore, to hold Matthew, Mark and Luke responsible for the three Gospels which now bear their names, and in their present form ? ' Utterances' would scarcely be a fitting title for the First Gospel as it now stands; the Second, with its precise and orderly arrangement,[1] is far from being a medley of ' Reminiscences ;' and the Third, the fullest, most varied and most finished of the three, is certainly not a ' Summary' of Pauline preaching. The titles do not cover the books. But we may say, if it is wished, that Matthew, Peter and Paul were sources of information, that Matthew's nameless Greek representative, Peter's interpreter Mark, and Paul's follower Luke, did commit that information to writing, and we may go further and say that our three Synoptic Gospels are ' according to ' Matthew and ' according to ' Mark and ' according to ' Luke ; but only in the sense in which we may say that ' Hamlet' is according to Saxo-Grammaticus, or that ' Faust' is according to Marlowe, or Calderon —or Job. And after all, as has been rightly said, it is of much less importance to know the name of a writer than to know the drift and value of what he says.

When and how did the fresh matter come in ? This, of course, must be largely matter for conjecture, but it

[1] Dr. Salmon (*Introduction to the New Testament*, p. 101, ed. iv.) contends that the Second Gospel shows a want of order *when compared with the Third*, whilst another apologist (Halcombe, *Gospel Difficulties*) maintains that the *chronological difficulties* of the latter can be explained only by transposing whole chapters!

is easy to conceive how, in a single generation, the tiny stream of pure tradition, parted into different channels, might quickly become swollen and coloured by tributaries of fanciful embellishment, of religious preconception, of party conflict, and yet be gathered at last in one settled and unquestioned course. Certain it is that in the second century the Gospels, largely in the form in which we now have them, were the common armoury of apologists and heretics ; by the fourth century had settled themselves into an orthodox Canon ; and at the time of the Reformation received the seal of final Protestant infallibility.

Note :—The oldest extant MS. of the Gospels cannot be placed higher than the fourth century. The oldest version (the Syriac Peshito) may have been made in the second century, but it does not now exist in its original form. The MSS. of the writings of the earliest Fathers rarely rise above the tenth century, and their citations from the New Testament, often made from memory and with little attempt at verbal exactness, are of uncertain value in textual criticism.

The Fourth Gospel stands so distinctly apart that it demands separate consideration. Happily we need not choose, as was once thought necessary, between the two positions that it is either from beginning to end a faithful record, or else throughout a work of pure invention. For it is possible to recognise a substratum of personal recollection and at the same time to detect and allow for the presence of super-added matter. That there is a foundation laid by the hand of a companion of Jesus, no one can seriously doubt. Several of the incidents which mark the personal relations of the Master to his followers are introduced in an easy, natural manner and seem to be genuinely real. What can be more artless and more life-like than the accounts of the calling of the first disciples, of the washing of the disciples' feet, of the running to the empty tomb? The references to the current hopes, beliefs and customs of the Jews and to the topography of Palestine are, with few exceptions, clear and accurate. It has been observed also[1] that the incidental indications of character, as for instance in Peter and Martha and Mary, correspond closely with the traits recorded by the other Evangelists. There are two passages at least which point to information received from an eye-witness.[2] All this may be allowed, without at the same time allowing that the Witness and the Writer are one.

I. The earliest date claimed for the Fourth Gospel is A.D. 80—90. It is therefore assumed by those who hold the Johannine authorship that the apostle in extreme old age, after long residence in a foreign country, wrote down his recollections of words and deeds from which he was divided by at least half a

[1] Gess, *Christi Person u. Werk.* 311.
[2] John xix. 35, xxi. 24. In the second passage, however, the 'disciple' who bears 'witness' is possibly the writer whose witness to the witness of his apostle-master now dead is attested by the Ephesian elders.

century and so gave us the work entirely from his own hand. Now the Witness of the Fourth Gospel, to be also the Writer, is at once too precise and too vague, too minute and too general, too explicit and too reserved. He is very exact, even after the lapse of fifty years, in his recollection of *days* (i. 29, 35, 43, ii. 1, iv. 40, xi. 6, xii. 1, 12), of *hours* (i. 39, iv. 6, 52, xix. 14), of particular *speakers* (vi. 8, xi. 16, xii. 4, xiii. 36, xiv. 5, 8, 22), of *number* (ii. 6, v. 5, vi. 13, xxi. 11), of *distance* (iv. 5, vi. 19, xi. 18, xxi. 8), of *weight* (xii. 3, xix. 39). But the hand which draws out the separate sections of the work with superfluous accuracy seems to be unable to connect them. The evidence is given circumstantially, but without sequence. The deponent can remember the details, but not the outline. It is as though a dramatist should have his Acts and Scenes before him in the most finished form and not be able to piece them. We do not ask for strict chronological order from the Synoptists; they are compilers only and they make the best they can of fragmentary records and floating traditions. But this is an original composition by the hand of a companion of Jesus. We ask that in submitting his facts he should have distinct knowledge of their order. If it be only an abridged narrative, a volume of selections and not a complete chronicle, we still expect that, with so powerful a memory to help him, the chapters shall show clear marks of detachment from the life of which they form a part. If the Fourth Gospel were solely a collection of isolated fragments, of interesting episodes, it would be another matter. But its author aims at more than this. He seeks to give to his work a biographical character. A companion and fellow-traveller, no one could better, or more easily, break the chain of events where he liked and show the severed links by definite notes of time and place. But it is just at these points of connection with the main line of the narrative that his reminiscences fail. He has no calendar to go by and no route to follow. "A feast of the Jews" is the conventional date ; Jerusalem, for the most part, the conventional scene. These Feasts and these Judæan ministries are the despair of the harmonists. To find room for a skeleton history of six Feasts, including three (perhaps four) Passovers, a public ministry which probably lasted one year is extended to two years and three months, and even to three years and six months.[1]

[1] It must not be supposed that the Fourth Gospel was written purposely to supply the omissions of the first three. In this case the writer would hardly have related the Cleansing of the temple, the Healing of the nobleman's son at Capernaum, the Feeding of the five thousand, the Walking on the sea, the Anointing at Bethany, and the Entry into Jerusalem. Moreover, some of his statements are historically at variance with the accounts given by the other Evangelists, and are occasionally to be preferred. And yet there is apparently no consciousness of any discrepancy. So far from completing the half-told tale, the Fourth Evangelist disturbs the chronology of the Synoptists, on many matters of supreme importance is as often silent and sometimes more obscure, professes only one aim in writing (xx. 31), and, where an opportunity for further explanation occurs (xxi. 25), speaks as though he were the sole writer.

§ II. The doctrine of the Fourth Gospel is not the doctrine of the first Three. It is no longer "the gospel of the kingdom" that is preached. Membership in the Kingdom is exchanged for the immediate incorporation with Christ of the individual soul.[1] The general call to repentance passes into something like the Pauline doctrine of Election. The spiritual man must be born from above;[2] he can receive nothing, except it have been given him from heaven;[3] the Son quickens whom he will;[4] that which the Father gives him shall come unto him;[5] no man can come unto him except the Father draw him;[6] he that is of God hears the words of God;[7] it is the Father who gives the shepherd his sheep;[8] not for the world but for these he prays;[9] everyone that is of the truth hears his voice.[10] The return of the King to his Kingdom, the Second Advent, is lost in the vaguer conception of the mission of the Comforter, and the promise of promotion in the Kingdom in the more distant assurance of resurrection in the last day.[11] The Holy Ghost becomes for the first time in Holy Scripture distinctly personal. The contrast between the Law and the Gospel is more strongly marked. There will be a truer worship than that of the temple;[12] there is a truer life than that which they thought to find in the Scriptures;[13] there is a truer bread than that which Moses gave.[14] The

[1] vi. 56. [2] iii. 3. [3] iii. 27. [4] v. 21. [5] vi. 37, xvii. 6, 9.
[6] vi. 44 (cf. 65). [7] viii. 47. [8] x. 29.
[9] xviii. 9. [10] xviii. 37. [11] vi. 39, 40, 44, 54. [12] iv. 21.
[13] v. 39. [14] vi. 32.

commandment of love is a new commandment,[1] the guidance of the Spirit will be a new revelation.[2] Disciples are no longer blindly obedient servants, but enlightened and trusted friends.[3] The Master himself may be addressed in prayer,[4] or prayer to the Father may be offered in his name.[5]

III. Still less are the Discourses of the Fourth Gospel the actual words of Jesus. They are profound, elaborate addresses, bearing mainly on the person and office of the speaker, addresses which the Jesus of the Synoptists could not have uttered. As we read them, it is difficult to resist the impression that it is really the writer who is speaking. Indeed sometimes the disguise of reported speech is hardly maintained ; the author's reflections grow more and more distinct ; the characters retire ; and that which began as a dialogue ends as a soliloquy. The point of transition is not always at first sight clear. Let the first Discourse, that with Nicodemus (ch. iii.), be taken as an example. The deflection may be at *v.* 6, or at *v.* 11, or at *v.* 16, but we cannot reach the end without feeling that the writer has drifted on the current of his own thoughts far away from the original scene.[6] The Discourse in Chapter Five is a long monologue, supposed at the

---

[1] xiii. 34. [2] xvi. 7, 13, xiv. 16, 26, xv. 26.
[3] xv. 15. [4] xiv. 13 (R.V.) [5] xvi. 24, 26.
[6] Similarly in iii. 27—36 no one can suppose that the words of the last six verses were really spoken by the Baptist. In xvii. 3, there is introduced, as part of the actual prayer, a passage which can only be explained as a reflection of the writer. Cf. the abrupt insertion of *v.* 12 in the same chapter. See also especially iv. 38.

beginning to be addressed to a band of hostile Jews, but it ends in silence, for there are none to hear or to reply. In the Sixth Chapter a simple figurative statement is forced into a literal acceptance and carried through stage after stage of needless confusion and misapprehension, to end at last in unnecessary rupture between the speaker and his hearers. It is difficult not to feel that the writer is indulging a love of paradox and mystery, the absence of which is one of the most marked traits in the character of his Master.[1] In the Eighth Chapter, especially, text and comment are

---

[1] For touches of mysticism, see xi. 49, 50, xix. 23, 34. and perhaps iv. 18, xix. 36.. With regard to the latter part of the sixth chapter, it may be confidently said that, if any reference to the Holy Communion had been intended, some mention of the rite itself would somewhere have been made. It is easy to say that the writer "living in the centre of Christian society does not notice the institution of a service which was part of the settled experience of Church life." But, if the words in question were in any way preparatory to the service, the service itself would hardly have been left unnoticed. The probability is that the connection never even occurred to the writer. With him, faith in Christ is incorporation with Christ. In the First Epistle it is to *have* the Son, in the Gospel it is to *eat and drink* the Son. It was a harsh but telling image for the expression of a difficult thought, the thought which is expressed more simply, though not so forcibly, in S. Paul's phrase (Rom. xiii. 14) ' Put ye on the Lord Jesus Christ.'

It may be observed, in passing, that, as the Books of the Prophets furnish the Synoptists with suggestions for incidents, so this writer finds starting-points for his arguments in certain facts related in the Books of the Law. Jacob's well, the brazen serpent, the manna, the smitten rock, the pillar of fire, are all introduced in successive chapters, iii.—viii.

closely entangled, whilst in the farewell Discourse extending over three chapters—xiv.—xvii.—the conditions of time and place compel us to see a very free expansion of original matter. And, looking back over the whole field, it cannot escape us that the tone of these Discourses is deliberately controversial, and that the controversy, from time to time, is stimulated and helped on by questions and objections which are unnatural, shallow, and sometimes childish.[1] " The Jews" are addressed at various times as if the same group were invariably present,[2] advancing and retiring with one united front. Where are the " gracious words " of him who drew and held the thronging crowds ? They are reserved for the chosen few whom the Father has given into his hand.

The unreality of the whole presentation in the Fourth Gospel is thus described by a careful student :— " The characters introduced play the same parts under different names. They act and speak in defiance of all recognised rule. They come and go and take one another's place, but why, or how, or what becomes of them, no one knows. Their dialogues produce only a medley of misunderstandings and misconstructions, of startling questions, awkward answers and ill-timed objections. The author's Nicodemus and Samaritan woman, his Pharisees and Jews and Greeks who file before us, make up types, not individuals, and Jesus

[1] ii. 20. iii. 4. iv. 11, 15. vi. 31, 52. vii. 35. viii. 33, 41, 52, 57, xiv. 8.
[2] vii. 23, viii. 12, 21, 22, 30, 31, 33, x. 24.

E

himself is rather an abstraction than a living being."[1] But the reader will gladly balance this severe language by the wise reminder of a more generous critic. " What wonder is it," he asks, " that in these our latter days, all thoughtful minds, whether in search of comfort from Christian truth, of instruction from Christian holiness, are turning by a natural instinct to the writings of the Apostle who taught us that God is Spirit, and that God is Love ?"[2]

In the Prologue to the Gospel—i. 1—18—the writer introduces a term which he assumes to be well known to his readers. It is the title *Logos*, the *Word*. The conception of the Thought or Will of God, hypostatised and acting visibly upon the world and upon men, was at that time, under various aspects, common to Palestinian and Hellenic systems of religious philosophy. It is from the Palestinian source, possibly, that the writer derives directly the idea of the *Word*, though he expresses it in the current Greek form λόγος. The novelty of his presentation lies, not in the doctrine of the *Logos*—that was widely spread—but in the identification of the *Logos* with Jesus. It is a new departure, giving an entirely new turn to speculative thought, when he declares that "the Word became flesh."

But it is to be observed that, having once presented the doctrine of the *Logos* under this new aspect, he leaves it as it stands without further mention. It is not even his main position. At the end of his work he

---

[1] Stap, *Études historiques et critiques*, p. 275.
[2] Stanley, *Sermons and Essays on the Apostolical Age.*

says expressly that his object is to prove that Jesus is the Christ, the Son of God.[1] He takes up narrower ground. His purpose all along has been, he says, to show that Jesus is the Messiah. If this be so, perhaps we may conclude, first, that the doctrine of the *Logos* was with him of secondary importance ; next, that it was introduced as a Preface which would be acceptable to all readers, whether under the influence of Hebraic, Philonean, or Gnostic teaching; and, lastly, that it must be viewed in close conjunction with the more local and more limited doctrine of the Jewish Messiah. The theological import of one doctrine must not be strained at the expense of the other. A Jew, yet often anti-Judaic, a Christian, yet necessarily anti-Hellenic, the writer adroitly seizes a term which from the time of Plato had been filled by different hands with different meanings and employs it, in a new conception, as a point of reconciliation between Judaism and Hellenism, between revelation and speculation, between historical fact and philosophical abstraction, between religious realism and religious idealism. The Word, the energising Will of God, stands, says the writer, in perpetual relationship to God, and, in a sense, is God. This Word, this Will, " became flesh" in Jesus Christ. But does he say that the Word in its totality became man ?[2] Did he not consider the Incarnation as one only of the

[1] xx. 31. cf. i. 20, 42, 50. iv. 26. vii. 26, 31, 43. ix. 22. x. 24.

[2] Justin in his *First Apology* speaks of Christ as incarnate διὰ λόγου θεοῦ; he is born of the Virgin διὰ δυνάμεως τοῦ λόγου; " the *Logos* sometimes personates a prophet, sometimes he speaks in the person of God, sometimes in the person of Christ,"

manfestations of that creative, indwelling Power which was in the world, and by which, he says, the world was made? Are the terms *Logos* and Christ to him co-extensive and convertible? Does he say Christ is God, ὁ θεός?[1] There are only three passages in the New Testament which seem in so many words to affirm the absolute deity of Christ. They are:—Acts xx. 28, "The church of God which he purchased with his own blood;" Titus ii. 13, "The glory of our great God and Saviour Jesus Christ; 2 Peter i. 1, "The righteousness of our God and Saviour Jesus Christ." In the first, for 'God,' many early MSS. read 'the Lord;' in the second the Revisers allow the alternative rendering, 'of the great God and our Saviour Jesus Christ,' and place it in the margin; and in the third they admit in the same way the translation, 'of our God and the Saviour Jesus Christ.'[2] S. Paul gives the best illustration of the lax and of the strict use of the word θεός, and at the same time the best correction, in 1 Cor. viii. 5, 6, "Though there be that are called gods, whether

(86, 43, 46, cf. 83.) See, however, *Apol.* ii. 8. On the other hand Weizsäcker (*Apostolisches Zeitalter*, p. 554) says very positively, "der geschichtliche Jesus ist der ganze Logos." Cf. Dorner, *Glaubenslehre*, ii. 394; but this writer's later exposition of the doctrine of the *Logos* is severely criticized by Gess (*Christi Person u. Werk*, 306—324).

[1] Those who argue that it would be Sabellian to say "the Word was ὁ θεός," that by the use of the article the distinction between the Father and the Son would be obscured, do not seem to hesitate to predicate ὁ ἀληθινὸς θεός of the Son in 1 John v. 20.

[2] In both passages the position and the determining force of ἡμῶν must be carefully considered.

in heaven or on earth ; as there are gods many, and lords many ;[1] yet to us there is one God, the Father, . . . and one Lord, Jesus Christ." See further Appendix III. and, for the use of θεός and ὁ θεός, Westcott, *Epp. of S. John*, 172.

It is sometimes said that the idea of the Word in Palestine and the idea of the Word in Alexandria were widely different, and, further, that Philo has no one clear and consistent view of the *Logos*. It is true that the *Logos* is sometimes conceived by Philo as existing independently, sometimes as immanent in the Divine Mind, but Zeller has shown that this variety of presentation arises from the necessity of his position. The perfect and infinite God cannot, by his theory, come into direct contact with finite and imperfect matter. To reconcile these opposites without this contact, the interposing medium must be identical with each and yet different from both. It must be at the same time personal and impersonal. Philo apparently saw the necessity for both notions, but did not perceive the impossibility of combining them. The same writer has shown that the Philonean doctrine of the *Logos* really had its root in the teaching of the Stoics. (*Die Philosophie der Griechen, iii. 2, p. 385*, quoted by Schürer. See also Tertullian, *Apology*, xxi., for direct reference to the *Logos* of Zeno.) For a comparison of the Hellenic with the Jewish-Christian Doctrine of the *Logos*, see Dorner,

[1] Cf. Ps. cxxxvi. 2, 3. John x. 35.

Doctrine of the Person of Christ, vol. i. pp. 120, 403, 4, Eng. Tr.[1]

VI. THE KINGDOM OF GOD.

The conception of a divinely appointed king involves the idea of a divinely constituted kingdom. Messiah's kingdom is the 'Kingdom of God.'[2] The phrase itself does not appear in prophecy, but the thought is sometimes disclosed.[3] By combining two typical passages—Jer. xxxi. 31—34 and Daniel vii. 13, 14—the spiritual and the material aspects of the universal kingdom are revealed.[4] It is at once an inner life and

[1] The doctrine of the Personality of the *Logos* prior to the Incarnation rests almost entirely on the expression ' πρὸς τὸν θεόν' in John i. 1; but personality implies individuality and consciousness, and, whatever the sense of the words may have been in the writer's mind, it is difficult to believe that he would have described individually-self-conscious-being by such a term as *Logos.* For *Logos* signifies pure *Thought, Reason, Will,* and these can only be thought of, can only subsist, in conjunction with a thinking, reasoning, willing subject.

[2] The alternative term 'Kingdom of Heaven' is peculiar to the First Gospel. The wider form, 'Kingdom of God,' occurs frequently in the Second and Third Gospels and occasionally in the First and Fourth. In Rabbinical language the term Heaven was often substituted for the name of God.

[3] See Hengstenberg, *History of the Kingdom of God,* Eng. Tr.; and, for typical passages, Is. xxxv. xlii. 1—16; Jer. xxiii. 5—8; Hos. xiv. 4—9; Joel ii. 32, iii. 9—21; Mic. v. 4; Zech. ii. 10, 11.

[4] It is true, as Reuss has observed (*Hist. de la Théologie Chrétienne* i. 179), that the sanctuary of Sion was still to be the centre of the world, that circumcision (Ezek. xliv. 9) was to be

an outward polity.   In the Apocrypha, though there is
no reference to Messiah personally, there is frequent
mention of a national restoration, political and religious.
The yoke of foreign oppression will be thrown off; the
Jews of the dispersion will return; hopes of general
forgiveness and sanctification are indulged; there is to
be a new rule of life and a new Jerusalem.   For
Messiah's empire, with Messiah's office, had again
shrunk to the limits of national ambition.   There are
traces of this contraction in the Gospels, even in the
forms into which the words of Jesus are thrown.   "Go
not into any way of the Gentiles, and enter not into any
city of the Samaritans."[1]   "I was not sent but unto
the lost sheep of the house of Israel."[2]   The morality
of the Gentiles is contrasted with the future morality of
the Kingdom, as though the distinction would remain.[3]
But it is not difficult, if we may trust the Evangelists,
to gather a wholly opposite intention from the lips of
the King himself.   "Many shall come from the east
and the west, and shall sit down with Abraham, and
Isaac, and Jacob, in the kingdom of heaven;"[4] the

the first condition of membership; but the idea of universality is
not necessarily, as he seems to think, excluded.   Cf. Ps. cxiii. 3.
Zeph. ii. 11.   Mal. i. 11.   The contractions and expansions of
the Messianic hope, with the varying fortunes of the nation, are
repeated in the narrower and wider views of the Kingdom, at one
time confined to the Holy Land and at another embracing the
world at large.   See Schürer, *Geschichte des Judischen Volkes*,
Part II. Vol. II. § 29.

[1] Matt, x. 5.   [2] Matt. xv. 24.   [3] Matt. v. 47, vi. 7, 32, xviii. 17.
[4] Matt. viii. 11.

" Gospel of the kingdom shall be preached in the whole world ;"[1] it is even said that, " The kingdom of God shall be taken away, and shall be given to a nation bringing forth the fruits thereof."[2]   In the Parables of the Kingdom there is the clearest foreshadowing of a world-wide sway.   The Sower's field is as large as the world itself ;[3] nothing can compete with the Kingdom's growth,[4] or resist its influence,[5] or escape its test.[6] As many as can be found are gathered to the Marriage Feast ;[7] the fruits withheld by native husbandmen will be rendered by strangers ;[8] the younger son will divide once more with his brother his Father's love.[9]

If Jesus took up the Baptist's cry, " The kingdom of heaven is at hand," it was in a different key.   The voice in the wilderness was an echo of the stern and mournful tone of later prophecy.   It is Jehovah Himself who is at hand.   The day beginning to break is a day of judgment—" it burneth as a furnace ;" "it is a day of wrath."   The worthless chaff and the fruitless tree are doomed to unquenchable fire.   The child of the desert was a true son of the prophets.   At the same time, if there was little consolation in his words, there was comfort in reserve.   The Baptist gave to his countrymen a new symbol.   For the proselyte's bath of Levitical purification, was substituted the penitent's baptism in token of moral cleansing.[10]   The frequent ceremonial

---

[1] Matt. xxiv. 14.   [2] Matt. xxi. 43. .   [3] Matt. xiii. 38.
[4] Matt. xiii. 32.   [5] Matt. xiii. 33.   [6] Matt. xiii. 47.   [7] Matt. xxii. 9.
[8] Matt. xxi. 41.   [9] Luke xv. 32.
[10] It has been contended that the baptism of Jewish proselytes

washings which cleansed from outward legal taint were
crowned by a single rite, administered once, in token
of enduring purity of heart. The "baptism of repentance" followed only upon confession of sin and
promise of amendment. To those who without repentance would adopt baptism as a wise precaution,
came the indignant "Vipers that ye are, who hath
warned *you?*" It was a startling and wholesome
lesson.

There was another touch of originality in the preaching of John. His message was for all. None need
despair. Outcasts from society and from the synagogue
might draw near; they would not be cast out of the
Kingdom. It was a bold stroke thus to ignore the
double ban. But in the boldness of the Baptist's
mission lay the chief bar to its success. The offer of
free pardon to the lawless is a shock to those who
administer the law. What they have bound no other
hand must loose. Therefore, if John gained the gratitude of one class, he lost the sympathy of another, and
that the more powerful. The work was good and bore
good fruit, but as a religious movement it failed. The
history of its failure is written in the First Gospel :—
"John came unto you in the way of righteousness, *and
ye believed him not :* but the publicans and harlots

was not known in ante-Christian times. For the facts and
arguments on the other side, see Schürer, *Geschichte*, &c., Part II.
Vol. II. § 31. Suggestions of baptismal cleansing may be gathered
from Ezek. xxxvi. 25. Zech. xiii. 1., and Isaiah i. 16 is quoted
by Justin as prophetic of Christian baptism.

believed him ; and ye, when ye saw it, did not even repent yourselves afterwards, that ye might believe him."[1] Whether the baptism was from heaven, or from men, they did not care sufficiently to say.[2]

How far the ministry in Judæa suggested the ministry in Galilee, it would be rash to conjecture, but that it made a deep impression, and exercised at first a strong influence, on the mind of Jesus, cannot be doubted. He hastens to the Baptist's side and at his hands receives baptism. The explanation given is that he submitted to the rite that he might "fulfil all righteousness." "Righteousness" in the Greek text can have only one meaning. It is "that which the law demands." Jesus, we are given to understand, submitted to baptism as a legal obligation. Now, in the first place, it was not a legal ordinance ; it stood on a footing altogether distinct from that of Levitical lustration ; it was the special symbol of a special intention. Nor was it meant to be a permanent institution under a new law. It was, on the Baptist's own shewing, a purely transitional rite, for it was to be followed by a superior baptism of spiritual fire.[3] Therefore, to put the position in the plainest terms, we are asked to believe that Jesus, who afterwards condemned nothing more strongly than mere ceremonial cleansing, allowed himself to go through an act which,

---

[1] Matt. xxi. 32.   [2] Matt. xxi. 27.
[3] Matt. iii. 11.   Luke iii. 16.   Cf. Acts i. 5.   xi. 16.   Mark x. 38.   Luke xii. 50.

in the eyes of those who beheld it, indicated intense moral effort, but was really for him a superfluous formality.

The alternative position we do not shrink from stating. Jesus freely accepted the "baptism of repentance."[1] It was for him, as for others, a termination and a starting-point; the ending of one period, the beginning of another. In deep self-searching he had found the secret of spiritual life. The light of a new principle breaks upon him. Moral purity, not legal purification, is the soul of religion. But legalism was not only the creed of his country and of his age, it had been the rule of his home and of his own early life. The Baptist was right; the voice in the wilderness was the echo of his own thought. Purity, not purification. God is able, even of Jordan's stones, to raise up spiritual children. The power of tradition, the power of early habit, are broken. In baptism he will announce to all a change of view and a new departure.

But the two spirits drawn together by a strong sympathy were soon to diverge. Beyond purity of life as a preparation for Jehovah's coming, John's preaching was not able to advance. The Kingdom of God was still to him a revived Theocracy. But in the mind of Jesus one thought developed another. The

---

[1] Μετάνοια does not invariably imply change of conduct. It is, primarily, a change of thought, an amended view of life, with a re-arrangement of its aims.

reign of purity in the soul is itself the expected Kingdom. It is thus that God is revealed and received. The pure in heart are more than blessed, they see God. The Kingdom was indeed " at hand," for it was " within."[1]

As they were not one in thought, neither were they one in method. The Baptist, though he held aloof from the temple and its ritual, from the Rabbis and their precepts, as a priest's son, followed legal usage ; but in the religious theory of Christ, externalism, though not excluded, was of little account. He did not, like John, baptize ; he did not, like him, enjoin fasting ; nor did he draw up special prayers for his followers. To do any of these things would be to sow again the seeds of formalism, after arresting its growth."[2]

That both were conscious of this divergence, is shown by their own words at a later date. The glad call of

[1] Luke xvii. 21. Cf. Matt. xi. 12. xii. 28, 34. xvi. 19. Mark ix. 47. xii. 34. Luke xiii. 29. xvi. 15. xxii. 16. xxv. 34. xxvi. 29. It must be borne in mind that the Kingdom is spoken of in the Gospels as both present and future, visible or invisible, according to its conception, at the moment, as an operation, or as a result.

[2] In the Fourth Gospel (iv. 1, 2) Jesus is said to have baptized through his first-chosen five disciples, and with a success which moved the envy of the Pharisees. But no hint of this is given in the Synoptic Gospels, and, in the sending forth of the Twelve, and afterwards of the Seventy, to baptize is not one of their instructions. That baptism, as a Christian institution, was ordained by Christ himself, is a doctrine which, for its Scriptural basis, rests only on the closing verse of the First Gospel, a verse

the gospel is to the stern preaching of the Baptist as
the gladness of pipe and dance compared with wailing
and beating of breasts.[1] He that is but little in the
kingdom of heaven is greater than the greatest amongst
the sons of women[2] because of his higher view of the
nature of the Kingdom. The Baptist in his turn lives
just long enough to doubt whether Jesus be the Christ,[3]
so little does the latter fulfil his own severe conception
of Messiah's work.[4] His disciples, if the writer of the
Fourth Gospel is to be followed, had once brought him
a jealous report of the popularity of Jesus,[5] and these
disciples in a dispute with the Jews as to baptism
(apparently whether that of John or that of Jesus was
the more effectual in purifying from sin) had already
contended for their master's honour.[6]

What then are the conditions of admission to the
Kingdom ? They may be gathered from various
utterances recorded by the Evangelists. Some are
stated negatively. Pious feeling[7] and good intentions[8]

which, apart from the fact that it belongs to the post-Resurrection
period, would on other grounds be open to suspicion. See
Appendix II. The correction of John iii. 22, 26, by iv. 2 shows
the hesitation that was felt in a later age in connecting the
institution of Christian baptism with Christ himself.
  [1] Matt. xi. 16, 17.   [2] xi. 11.   [3] xi. 3.
  [4] "He saw no axe or fan in his hand. He heard reports of
deeds of mercy, and of gracious words spoken unto the poor, but
he heard no reports of deeds of judgment." Bruce, *The
Kingdom of God*, p. 81.
  [5] John iii. 26.   [6] John iii. 25.   [7] Matt. vii. 21.
        [8] Luke ix. 62.

count for nothing. The rich may find the way barred by their own wealth.[1] Similar obstacles may arise from allowable aims,[2] from natural appetites,[3] even from innocent affections.[4] The leading positive condition is self-devotion, or faith. Faith is man's final answer to the call divine. Faith is the soul's, "Here am I ; for thou calledst me." This ready response to a rightful and mastering claim is the pass-word of the Kingdom. Faith is no shibboleth learned in time by stammering lips. It is an expansion of being in the presence of supreme goodness, a spiritual grasp which will never let go such truth as it can hold. Sooner than be denied it will move mountains,[5] and come at its desire by a kind of violence to take it by force.[6] To such impetuous knocking the Kingdom lifts up at once its everlasting doors.

'The Gospel of the Kingdom' is the announcement of a new principle of life in the individual, of a new rule of conduct in society, of a new soul-relationship to God. An attempt is made in the following pages to gather from the words of Jesus himself this system of divine order under the three heads of Moral Reform, Social Reform, and Spiritual Reform.

[1] Mark x. 24.　　[2] Matt. vi. 33.　　[3] Mark ix. 47.　　[4] Luke xviii. 29
[5] Matt. xvii. 20.　　　[6] Matt. xi. 12.

"Hoc est Christum cognoscere, beneficia ejus cognoscere."—*Melancthon.*

"A man's 'religion' consists not of the many things he is in doubt of and tries to believe, but of the few he is assured of, and has no need of effort for believing."—*Carlyle.*

"Why is the faith of the favoured few so unintelligibly orthodox, and that of the people at large, if they are Christians at all, so intelligible and so simply expressed?"—*T. Mozley.*

CHAPTER II.

Moral Reform.

I. QUALITIES REQUIRED IN MEMBERS OF THE KINGDOM.

CONSCIOUSNESS OF IMPERFECTION ;
Matt. v. 3. Luke xvii. 10.

SORROW THEREAT ;
Matt. v. 4.

CRAVING FOR UPRIGHTNESS ;
Matt. v. 6.

GENTLENESS ;
Matt. v. 5 ; xi. 29.

PITY ;
Matt. v. 7 ; xviii. 33 ; xxiii. 23. Luke x. 37.

PURITY ;
Matt. v. 8 ; xii. 35.

PEACEABLENESS ;
Matt. v. 9. Mark ix. 50.

PATIENCE ;
Matt. v. 39, 40, 41. Luke viii. 15 ; xviii. 29 ; xxi. 19.

HUMILITY ;
Luke xiv. 11. Matt. xviii. 4; xi. 29.

F

CHARITY ;

Matt. xxii. 37—39. Luke x. 37.

TOLERANCE ;

Matt. vii. 1 ; xiii. 30. Mark ix. 40. Luke ix. 55.

PERSEVERANCE ;

Luke ix. 62 ; xiv. 34. Mark iv. 5, 17. Matt. x. 22.

JUSTICE ;

Luke xi. 42 ; xvi. 10.

FORGIVINGNESS ;

Matt. vi. 15. Mark xi. 25.

TRUTHFULNESS ;

Matt. v. 37. Mark vii. 22.

LIBERALITY ;

Matt. v. 42. Luke xi. 41 ; xii. 33.

DECISION ;

Matt. vi. 24. Luke ix. 62.

TEMPERANCE ;

Matt. xxiv, 49. Luke xxi 34.

SELF-DENIAL.

Matt. xvi. 25. Mark ix. 43. Luke xiv. 33.

II. The righteousness of the Kingdom is not a Pharisaic obedience to the letter of the Law, but an honest interpretation of its spirit. Under this interpretation :—

1. The commandment against murder becomes a commandment against murderous anger — the blind, unreasoning anger which under other circumstances would result in murder.

Matt. v. 21, 22.

2. The commandment which forbids adultery to the married state forbids also the adulterous gaze—the deliberate gaze which only for lack of opportunity falls short of actual adultery.

Matt. v. 28.

3. The love which makes the neighbour another self, and the stranger a neighbour, will find even in an enemy something to speak well of—perhaps to love.[1]

Matt. xxii. 39. Luke x. 37. Matt. v. 44.

4. A so-called religious duty is never to be allowed to precede, or to be substituted for, a plain moral duty. To do this is to wear the actor's mask and to make of real life a passing play.

Matt. v. 23. Mark vii. 11; xii. 40. Matt. xxiii. 23.

5. The value of a moral action must be measured, first, by its motive ; then by the means and capacities of the agent; then, if at all, by the resulting act.

Matt. x. 42 xiv. 8.

---

[1] This extension of love from self outwards is sometimes thought to be an impossible ideal. The following considerations are suggested :—

a. We love the neighbour more than we suspect. In danger, or distress, or in the hour of death, our kinder feelings have freer play.

b. We do not really *love* ourselves. We are careful and thoughtful for ourselves, believe in ourselves, are ready to defend ourselves, are hopeful about ourselves. We are asked to do no less, *and no more*, to the neighbour.

c. To the enemy we can often allow that which in all fairness we are sometimes obliged to refuse to ourselves—a charitable construction.

[In short, the Morality of the Kingdom lies in a standard of right feeling as well as in a rule of right action. For instance, the possession of such virtues as truth, justice, purity, honesty is to be tested, not only by outward conduct, but by the degree of desire within for whatsoever things are true, just, pure, honest.]

Note.—It is not pretended that the Morality here proposed is for the present day complete. A great deal of our modern virtue is resistance to modern vice. Before we maintain that Christ's ethical code is defective, we must ask what were the ills and evils which it was intended to meet. It has been contended that Christianity passes over the important duties of unselfish parental forethought, and of consideration for dumb animals. Zealous reformers of drunkenness are also distressed to find how little is said about the use of intoxicating drink. But is it reasonable to look into the Gospel for any particular anticipation of nineteenth-century depravity bred by hard and unhealthy conditions of life which did not then exist? Why preach parental forethought to a people whose system of education and of family-maintenance was perfect, or consideration for dumb animals to those who had already learnt it from their Law,[1] or, in the matter of temperance, the special need of resistance to

[1] Cf. Exod. xxii. 30, xxiii. 19. Levit. xxii. 27, 28. Deut. xxii. 7, 10, and see especially Philo's treatise (translated by Friedländer under the title Über die Philanthropie des mosaischen Gesetzes), with his interesting comments on the foregoing passages.

a temptation which was scarcely known? If the necessity of a sense of responsibility, of mercy, of self-control, is insisted on, that is all we can expect, and, if we cannot apply the broad moral principle to each case of conduct as it arises, the fault is only our own.

CHAPTER III.

Social Reform.

Members of the Kingdom purify and enlighten society by an unconscious self-diffusion.

> Matt. v. 13, 14, 16. Mark iv. 21. Luke xi. 33.

By free intercourse and wide courtesy they practically ignore the distinctions of class. They do not take conspicuous rank over even the most degraded.

> Matt. v. 47. xxi. 31.

At the same time an impossible equality is not required. Those who sit on 'Moses' seat' have authority; those who rule over 'ten cities' have power; those who sit on 'twelve thrones' have honour; of those to whom much is "committed," much will be asked. But the selfish and exclusive enjoyment of mere title—'Rabbi,' 'Father,' 'Master'—is condemned. And he is the greatest who is great enough to serve.

> Matt. xxiii. 2. Luke xix. 17. Matt. xix. 28. Luke xii. 48.
> Matt. xxiii. 8, 9; xx. 27.

In the Kingdom poverty is neither an obstacle nor a reproach.[1]

> Matt. vi. 19, 25, 33. Luke xii. 15, 23; xvi. 22. Mark xii. 42.

[1] The most prominent 'fool' in the Gospel narrative is a restless capitalist (Luke xii. 20).

Riches, on the other hand, are not only misleading, perishable and unsatisfying, but are often an obstruction to the acceptance of truth. Far from being hoarded up, they should be used in relieving the wants of the poor, material and spiritual. Not the possession but the ill-getting or ill-using of money is condemned.

Matt. xii. 22 ; vi. 19. Luke xii. 23 ; vi. 24; xii. 15.
Mark x. 23, 25. Matt. xix. 21. Luke xii. 33; xvi. 9.

To help the poor is one of the fruits and proofs of amendment ; to neglect them is to neglect the Master himself.

Matt. xix. 21. Luke xix. 8. Matt. xxv. 42.

Nor must kindly effort be compounded for by a money-payment. The hungry must be fed, the naked clothed, and the stranger welcomed by the giver's hands, the sick and the prisoner visited in person. Moreover, true almsgiving is no outside act, but the parting with some dear desire within. Those who give up their own to enrich the common good, enjoy more than their own, for they enjoy a common wealth.

Matt. xxv. 35, 36. Luke xi. 41 ; xviii. 29, 30. Cf. Matt. v. 5.

Selfish ambition should be checked. The only gate to honour is humility.

Luke x. 20. Matt. xviii. 1, 3, 4.!; xx. 25, 26 ; xxiii. 11, 12.

There must be a like self-restraint in pleasure and amusement. Their abuse will waste the life and choke the heart. But, short of this, none of the sober gaieties of simple Eastern life are forbidden, or declined.

Luke xv. 13 ; viii. 14.

The hospitable will find their best guests amongst those who have few friends and nothing to give in return.

Luke xiv. 12.

Questions of legal right are best settled out of court, but where the law comes in it must be cheerfully obeyed.

Luke xii. 15. Matt. xxii. 21 ; xvii. 24 ; xxvi. 52.

Children have their place in the Kingdom. And children they must never wholly cease to be in after life to retain their place.

Matt. xviii. 2, 3, 10 ; xxi. 16. Mark x. 14.

The support of parents by the children is their first duty. In no higher way can they honour them, or God.

Mark vii. 10—13.

Persistent offenders should be remonstrated with, rebuked, presented, perhaps expelled ; the repentant cannot too often be forgiven, and forgiveness must be from the heart.

Matt. xviii. 15, 16, 17. Luke xvii. 3. Matt. xviii. 22, 35.

One offence is excepted. To place occasions of sin in the way of the young or of the weak is to deserve the punishment of ignominious death.

Luke xvii. 1, 2.

Note.—Here too it would be unreasonable to ask that the precepts of the Gospel should anticipate and meet modern social difficulties. It has been argued that improvidence is suggested, if not actually inculcated, that poverty has been glorified and exalted to the dignity of a virtue ; (Matt. vi. 25). But, because overthought for the morrow is deprecated, is fore-thought therefore discouraged ? If there is a time for leaving purse and scrip behind, is it not allowed that there is also a time for taking both, and a sword as well ? (Luke ix. 3 ; x. 4 ; xxii. 36). So too with riches. The point enforced is that a man's life con-sists not in the abundance of the things which he possesses ; (Luke xii. 15). In a particular case it might be the wisest course to part with unearned wealth and to begin the world again ; (Mark x. 21). But there are several parables and sayings bearing on the use of money which are not opposed to the con-clusions of economists as to the beneficial value of money employed as capital ; (Matt. xxv. 27. Luke xvi. 11. Mark x. 30. Luke xix. 23). Exhortations to alms-giving could not easily pauperise a people amongst whom those only were poor who were unable to work, to whom daily labour was part of the divine command, and with whom technical instruction was one of the first elements of education.

CHAPTER IV.

Spiritual Reform.

I. The New Covenant is not a new religion. It fills up the outline of the ancient Law.

> Matt. v. 17.

II. The substance of the spiritual law is, like heaven and earth, imperishable. It is, in its principle, the love of God and the love of man.

> Matt. v. 18. Luke xvi. 17 ; xxii. 37, 39.

But the ceremonial law stands on a different footing. The Sabbath, for instance, is a means, not an end.

> Mark ii. 27 (cf. John vii. 23).

The Temple itself, the work of half a century, might be destroyed and left desolate, but for the building of the true church on spiritual foundations even three days would suffice. The distinction between clean and unclean food is blotted out. All meats are made clean.

> Matt. xxiii. 38 ; xxvi. 61 ; xxvii. 40. ⁓ Mark vii. 19.

Ceremonial ablutions are pronounced to be indifferent, as resting only on the traditions of men.

> Matt. xv. 3. Cf. xxiii. 25, 26.

These traditions are heavy burdens grievous to be borne, whereas the yoke of God's will rightly understood is easy and the burden light.

> Matt. xxiii. 4; xi. 30.

To allow that the offering of the heart stands before the sacrifice of the altar is at least to be not far from the Kingdom of God.

Mark xii. 34. Cf. Matt. ix. 13 ; xii. 7.

In fact Judaism on the side of legalism is a worn and threadbare garment not to be patched with the new cloth of Christianity. It is an old wine-skin too weak for the new wine of new doctrine.[1]

Mark ii. 21. Matt. ix. 16. Luke v. 36.

Marriage is recalled to its first idea of spiritual one-ness, the spiritual attraction of two personalities into one life. The Mosaic permission of divorce on certain grounds was therefore a forced relaxation. The exten-

[1] At the same time the conservative teaching attributed to Christ on the ceremonial side ought not to be overlooked. To annul one of the least of the law's commandments is to be least in the kingdom ; the scribes are to remain in Moses' seat ; lepers who have been healed are still required to conform to the ritual of the priests ; not a word is said as to the abolition of the sabbath (cf. especially Matt. xxii. 20) or of circumcision, or of any festival, or even of any sacrifice (as to this last, see Matt. v. 23, 24.) There is the same perplexing contradiction between the Christ who is the associate of the Baptist in proclaiming the Kingdom, and the Christ who ranks him below the lowest grade in the Kingdom ; between the Christ who comes eating and drinking, discourages fasting and extols the married state, and the Christ who fasts in the wilderness and approves, if he does not enjoin, the ascetic, celibate life. (Compare Mark i. 14, 15 with Matt. xi. 11, and Matt. v. 3, xi. 19, Mark ii 18, Matt. xix. 5 with Matt. iv. 2, xvii. 21, Mark x. 21, Luke xvi. 9, vi. 20, xii. 33, xiv. 26, Matt. xix. 12.) The variations are possibly due to the Essene or anti-Essene tendencies of the first compilers of the oral tradition.

sion of this permission by a certain school to " every cause" is still more to be condemned. ·Henceforth the valid justification of divorce shall be adultery, and adultery only.[1]

Matt. xix. 4, 5.   Cf. Gen. i. 27 ; ii. 24.   1 Cor. vi. 16.
Matt. xix. 3, 9.

The prayer of the closet is better than ostentatious prayer in a public place at an appointed hour. It should not be in many words often repeated. A general feeling of dependence upon God is better than a special enumeration of wants.

Matt. vi. 6, 7, 8. ; vii. 11.

As an example of how much may be said in few words, a form of prayer is given :—

" Father, Hallowed be thy name. Thy kingdom come. Give us day by day our daily bread. And forgive us our sins ; for we ourselves also forgive every one that is indebted to us. And bring us not into temptation."

Luke xi. 2.

At the same time, though ' much speaking ' is reproved, much praying is encouraged. Intercessory prayer is especially enjoined. Over-anxiety about personal necessities is deprecated. [Prayer is never imposed as an exercise, or act of duty. It is part of

---

[1] Adultery, it has been argued, *ipso facto* breaks the spiritual bond, and divorce has already taken place. In the case of a mixed marriage between a Christian and a heathen, contracted before conversion, S. Paul in 1 Cor. vii. 15 allows separation, but, apparently, it is to be *separation*, not *divorce*.

the free play of a healthy soul ; it cannot be forced.
' Out of the overflow of the heart the mouth speaketh.'⟧

Matt. vii 7. Luke xviii. 1. Matt. xxvi. 41. ; v. 44.
Luke xvi. 27. Matt. ix. 38. Luke x. 2. Matt. vi. 34 ; xii. 35.

In alms-giving and in fasting, as in prayer, there
must be purity of intention and simplicity in action.
Let a man give and not remember it, let him fast and
not proclaim it.

Matt. vi. 3, 17.

A disciple's word is as solemn and as binding as an
oath, and more reverent.

Matt. v. 34, 37.

True piety is tested, like a tree, by its fruit, or, like
a house, by its foundation. Pretence of piety will in
the end be unveiled.

Matt. vii. 18, 24. Luke xii. 1, 2.

Filial imitation is the supreme motive. The children
of the heavenly Father will feel and act kindly because
He is kind ; will be merciful, even as He is merciful ;
will, in their measure, be perfect, even as He is perfect.[1]
This spiritual bond is stronger and closer than any tie
of human relationship.

Matt. v. 44. Luke vi. 36. Matt. v. 48. Luke viii. 21.

The Father's love is the supreme object. To this
the heart turns as to hidden treasure. This is the sole
aim of spiritual sight and of spiritual service.

Matt. vi. 21, 22, 24.

---

[1] This is the ' moral maximum,' rising high above the ' moral
minima' of legal obedience.

There is a Providence which watches with a Father's care over every want. [God is not *as* a Father, He *is* our Father. The announcement of this affinity, involving as it does spontaneous, reciprocal love between Father and Child—this is the central truth of the Gospel.]

Matt. x. 30; vi. 26. Luke xxi. 18; xxii. 35.

There is a holy spirit given by the Father to his children. There are also alien, hostile spirits ready to possess his heart.

Luke xi. 13   Matt. xii. 45.

To be kind to the unthankful, never despairing, is to be the son of the Most High who is good to all.

Luke vi. 35.

A gift may be small, if the love be great. For love's sake also great sins are forgiven. A gift without love is meet for no altar.

Matt. x. 42.   Luke vii. 47.   Matt. v. 24.

Inward graces and outward opportunities are loans which may be enlarged by use and must be accounted for. To neglect them is to lose them. At the same time there is a sense in which life is well lost, for there is one life that must be parted with that another may be gained.

Matt. xxv. 4, 14, 29.   Luke xiii. 8; ix. 24.

Persecution for righteousness' sake is to be expected, even welcomed. A man may have to face it even in his own household. He need not be anxious as to his defence. The spirit that is in him will speak for him. Nothing from without can hurt his soul.

Matt. v. 12 ; x. 36, 19, 20, 28.

Occasions of sin, causes of stumbling, must be removed, let the pain be what it may. This self-discipline is a purifying fire.

Matt. v. 29. Mark ix. 49.

In proportion to knowledge of divine law is the guilt of disobedience and its punishment.

Luke xii. 47, 48.

At the same time special afflictions in this life are no proof of special sinfulness.

Luke xiii. 2, 4.

To the sinful God is merciful :—

1. Not until the tree of a human life has become irreclaimable and hurtful to the ground is it cast out of the vineyard.

Luke xv. 3, 8, 11, 7.

2. The door of the Kingdom is narrow and every nerve must be strained to enter it. But only at the end of time is the door closed, and only to those who would seek admission under false pretence.

Luke xiv. 24 ; xiii. 25, 26.

3. Again, the Kingdom is a divine feast to which all are invited. Those only are forbidden to taste who have no taste for it.

Luke xiv. 24.

Salvation is a healthy condition of life ; life preserved from, and protected against, sin.

Luke xix. 9. Matt. xviii. 11 ; i. 21.

Every command of God is deducible from the commandment of love. The right path of action is therefore always plain.

Matt. xxii. 40; vii. 12.

In the spiritual, as in the natural world growth is secret and slow and shows stages of development. Spiritual effects can only follow from spiritual antecedents. Ripened fruit presupposes labour and culture.

Mark iv. 26; Matt. vii. 16.

The heart is a seed-bed of truth, and of error; a treasury of good, and of evil.

Matt. xiii 19; Mark viii. 17; Matt. xii. 35; Mark vii. 21; Luke vi. 45.

Rest of soul can only come to those who have learned to overcome the restlessness of anger and of pride.

Matt. xi. 29.

The greatest hindrance to truth is the bigotry of its friends. For men love that to which their taste has grown. The old, they say, is good. Or, on the other hand, truth may suffer from the innovations of official zeal. But its final triumph is assured.

Luke v. 39; Matt. xv. 6; x. 26.

Self-complacent pride stands on a lower level before God than self-accusing shame.

Luke xviii. 9.

The sons of the light may learn a lesson in forethought from the prudent sons of the world. Nor is it impossible to be wise and yet simple.

Luke xvi. 8. Matt. x. 16.

In all spiritual effort faith is the lever which uproots and removes every obstruction.

Luke xvii. 6.

The hope of immortality lies in the broad fact that God is not only the source but the object of imparted life.

Luke xx. 38 ; x. 25—27.

Of the future state little can be said. It is enough to know that the sons of the resurrection are still the sons of God.[1] They shall shine forth as the sun in the kingdom of their Father.

Luke xx. 36. Matt. xiii. 43.

For himself he asks that they will trust God in him.[2] Faith at its highest is as strong as love. Let them rise up and follow, and he will lead them to God. That which he asks is not so much attachment to a person as devotion to a cause.

Matt. x. 40, 37. Mark viii. 34. Matt. xix. 29, compared with Luke xviii. 29. But cf. also Matt. x. 32, 40 ; vii. 23 ; xviii. 5 ; Luke ix. 57 ; x. 16.

———

["Loyalty to Goodness" is a fine definition of faith which we owe, perhaps, to the author of *Ecce Homo*.

[1] "Aus dem Glauben an Gott erwächst die Hoffnung des ewigen Lebens. Kinder Gottes sind unsterblich." Pestalozzi, quoted by Gess.

[2] It has been remarked that the one instance in the Synoptical Gospels in which Christ speaks of Himself as the object of faith is in the passage on childlike humility in Matt. xviii. 5 ; "Whoso shall receive one such little child receiveth me."

G

"Faith has its life in a certain moral temper," says another writer not less happily. Faith, to our mind, is a daring dependence on divine control. It is not knowledge, for it is not gathered from outward evidence; it is not belief, for it is not grounded on outward testimony. It has an evidence and a testimony, but they are within. It is confidence in God, with a derived confidence in self. It is not the perfect apprehension of a complete system of truth, but the practical, realising grasp of that portion, be it much or little, which comes into view. This is the faith of the Gospels, often unreasoning, but always unerring.

Faith is equal only to certain plain demands made upon it in its own domain. It feels, by a kind of immediate knowledge, and obeys, by a kind of instinctive devotion, the eternal principles of right; it grasps, as far as it can, and acts upon, certain divine realities; but it cannot rightly be called upon to give any answer to the arguments and conclusions of human thought. Questions of historical fact or of doctrinal definition may be matters of pious, if transient, belief, but they are not, and cannot be, matters of faith and ought to be addressed to another faculty. Adherence to God is one thing, and assent to theological propositions about God is another. "Men may dispute," says Goethe, "about knowledge, because it can be widened, corrected; but not about faith."

Faith, then, is a principle of right action, not a certain mental disposition towards a given creed. It has no Articles. The attempt to take advantage of the ambiguity of the term and to force faith into the province of belief, of intellectual assent, has led to many confusing definitions and mischievous applications.

"Faith," says Newman (*University Sermons*), "is content with weaker evidence than Reason." And again, "It need not be weakness or rashness, if upon a certain presentiment of mind we trust to the fidelity of testimony offered for a revelation." "Faith," says Pearson, "is assent unto that which is credible, as credible"—*i.e.* (Wace, *Bampton Lect.* III.), "assent on the ground of testimony." "Faith," writes Tillotson, "is an assent of the mind to something as revealed by God." "Faith," thinks Mozley (*Bampton Lect.* IV.), "is the faculty to trust an argument," or "a permanent and hereditary belief by a natural law of transmission ;" (*Lect.* V.) "Faith," contends Liddon (*Bampton Lect.* VI.), "is a new sense of spiritual truth with which man has been endowed by grace."

No wonder is it if faith so overstrained has passed out of active allegiance into passive acquiescence and lies at last buried under mountains which it once moved. But not without first breaking from time to time into that mad violence of action which follows disordered thought. To the doctrine that correct theological opinions are essential to salvation, and that theological error necessarily involves guilt, "may be distinctly traced," says Lecky, "almost all the sufferings that Christian persecutors have caused, almost all the obstructions they have thrown in the path of human progress; and those sufferings have been so grievous, that it may be reasonably questioned whether superstition has not often proved a greater curse than vice, and that obstruction was so pernicious, that the contraction of theological influence has been at once the best measure and the essential condition of intellectual advance." (*History of European Morals,* vol. i.) This is the parable which history takes up against religion. "Superstition" and "obstruction" and the scorching fires of "persecution" mark the passage of faith from trust in God and loyalty to goodness into trust in arguments about God and loyalty to a creed.]

Note.—Under this head of Spiritual Reform, it must be admitted, there is more room for reasonable objection. We may go further and say that there are few things in history more lamentable than the fact that, as an effect of Christ's spiritual teaching, some of the worst inventions of pre-Christian superstition were gathered up, sanctioned and established as matter of Christian faith. Side by side with the purer vision of the Father of all Good rose the dark shape of the Author of all Evil, and beneath the walls of the new Jerusalem, as of the old, lay the fearful imagery of the valley of Gehenna. It has been urged that in Palestine the belief in Satan and hell and demons and demoniacal possession was not indigenous, that it was never anything more than a superstition of the common people, never received any religious sanction and was never seriously referred to in any authoritative Jewish writing. This is for the most part true, but, after making the fullest possible allowance for later additions, it is difficult to separate from the words and actions of Jesus all reference to a personal devil, to possession by unclean spirits, to a place of final torture. Still, it is not so much to the rude poetic imagery of that day as to the studied dogmatic literalism of after ages that we owe the horrors, cruelties, and impositions which flowed into Christendom from Jewish demonology and poisoned for centuries the springs of religious life.

"It has been the misfortune of Churches, that, unlike States, there has been on all sides equally a disposition either to assume the existence in early days of all the later principles of civilisation, or else to imagine a primitive state of things which never existed at all."— *Stanley*.

" Supposing other things equal, the superstition of a nation must always bear an exact proportion to the extent of its physical knowledge."—*Buckle*.

CHAPTER V.

The Kingdom and the World.

PART I.

True religion, like other forms of truth, may be too pure and too simple to be at once acceptable. A new faith had sprung from the lap of Judaism—born of her, but strong with independent life. It yearned for a freer air, and fled from the hands of the priest and of the rabbi to the mountain-side and the lake. Full of sympathy, of love, of reverence, it threw itself trustfully on nature and humanity and God. But men were not yet wise enough to enter the Kingdom as little children, and they soon lost the leading of the heavenly child. Christianity in its first revelation was religion in its purest and most spiritual form, and for that reason to the eyes which hailed it it was only half revealed. We often wonder why it is that, in social and political development, visions of truth hang in the air long before they are fully comprehended and followed. Is it not because the correlative organ of sight, in the mass of men, is not yet developed? " The light shineth in the darkness; and the darkness apprehended it not." "How much," asks Ruskin, "how much of a man does a serpent see?" And how much, we may say, of a new religion, or even of a new phase in an old religion, do its first converts see? To Jewish and Gentile believers alike the divine vision was not, and could not be, as perceptible as it is now, and until it had been grossly materialised was not, to most minds, perceptible at all. And this is the explanation of externalism, of concrete expression, in worship and belief. The range of sight is limited and its power defective. The eye is weak and sees parts only of the whole and sees them wrongly. Therefore we need not quarrel with past ages for being superstitious and for corrupting and distorting the faith that was in them. They materialised it and clothed it in order to see it.[1] In fact there can be no revelation in the sense of instant apparition. Religious truth grows on us as we grow to it.

There have been many ingenious theories as to the original sources of the Christian religion. And by the Christian religion the theorists too often mean the whole doctrinal and ceremonial medley which now goes by that name. This they take in hand, unravel the various threads and follow them back, correctly enough, to early religious and philosophical systems outside the Christian Church. But Christianity native to the soil of Palestine

---

[1] " Is not all worship whatsoever a worship by symbols, by *eidola*, or things seen? Whether *seen*, rendered visible as an image or picture to the bodily eye; or visible only to the inward eye, to the imagination, to the intellect: this makes a superficial, but no substantial difference."—Carlyle, *The Hero as Priest.*

is one thing, and Christianity weighted with alien grafts is quite another. The Christian faith grew, as it could only grow, out of the one ground which was able to produce it. Like any other resultant from antecedent forces, it has its heredity; and that heredity lies in the religion of the Jew. " Do men gather grapes of thorns, or figs of thistles?" Only from the nation which had cherished faithfully the thought of the One God could come forth the idea of the One Father; only from a people closely knit together, as no other people had ever been united, could come forth the conception of universal brotherhood. The thought and language of law and psalm and prophecy flow on without break or violence in the preaching of Jesus.[1] To the Jew the Gospel ought to have been acceptable, for it was the open flower of his own faith, rewarding centuries of growth. It was part of his own history, a stage in the evolution of his own life. It preserved the transmission of those influences which had led him in the desert, settled him in his inheritance, upheld the throne of his kings, anointed his priests, and inspired his sacred books. And indeed at first the holy city found no difficulty in

[1] Cf. the remarkable statement of Hegesippus as late as A.D. 150 in *Euseb. H. E.* iv. 22. "'Εν ἑκάστῃ πόλει οὕτως ἔχει ὡς ὁ νόμος κηρύττει καὶ οἱ προφῆται καὶ ὁ Κύριος." " In each city it is as the law and the prophets and the Lord proclaim." The not less remarkable statement in Acts xxi. 20 concerning the "myriads among the Jews which *believed*" and yet remained "zealous for the law," shows how little must at first have been presented by Christian teachers incompatible with Jewish faith and ceremonial observance.

making room for the new religious school. Where
synagogues abounded, one more congregation would
excite little attention. Jesus himself, because of his
bolder attitude, had fallen under the displeasure of the
ecclesiastical power, which dreaded schism, and of the
civil power, which feared sedition, but his followers
might hold him in their hearts as Messiah and remain
unmolested as before. And this they did for several
years, attending the temple worship, observing the
hours of prayer and the sacred festivals, and "having
favour with all the people."[1]   Even occasional attempts
at public action after the example of their Master were,
after warning, allowed to pass unpunished.[2] Afterwards, by degrees, the foreign Jews claimed a larger
share, first, in the alms, and then in the administration,
of the new church at Jerusalem.[3]   At last, with the
death of Stephen, the seed of the parent plant was
shaken out by persecution and took strange forms of
growth in other soils.

And here a difficulty presents itself.   Could the Jews
of Judæa, left to themselves, have developed to its
perfect fulness their own unfolding creed?[4]   Would
they have allowed the gospel which the Christ preached
to "change the customs which Moses delivered?"
Must we say, as Carlyle said of Arius, that, if afterwards the Ebionite had won, "Christianity would have

---

[1] Acts ii. 47.   [2] iv. 21.   v. 40.   [3] vi. 1, 8.   viii. 2.
[4] A thoughtful discussion of this question, discovered too late
to be of any service here, may be found in Stap's *Études historiques et critiques*, 3rd ed. 1891, pp. 49, 50.

dwindled into a legend ?" If so, it was well that the
foreign elements should come in. But if, on the other
hand, the " Grecian Jews," as they are called in Scripture, with their freer sympathies, did that which the
zealots of Palestine would never have done, how far did
they unduly enlarge that which their co-religionists as
unduly contracted ? If there were independent centres
of Christian teaching far away from Jerusalem ; if in
a single city, as in Corinth, in the earlier days of
S. Paul, there were three distinct parties besides the
apostle's own adherents ;[1] if, in another, as in Ephesus,
the "disciples" of John were scarcely distinguished
from those of Jesus ;[2] if it was allowable for the same
man to repudiate the Law, and, on occasion, without
scruple to obey it ;[3] if to deny the doctrine of the
resurrection of the dead did not entail loss of membership in a Christian community ;[4] where, and with
whom, was "the faith once delivered to the saints?"
If certain that " came from James" with anti-Pauline
teaching were "Judaisers," was not Paul himself, with
his Pharisaic logic, his Rabbinical rhetoric, a Judaiser
also ? To the sum of Catholic doctrine Jerusalem
contributed much, but Antioch and Ephesus and
Alexandria more. Where are we to set up the
barriers ? What are they to embrace, and what are
they to exclude ?

[1] 1 Cor. i. 12.   [2] Acts xviii. 25. xix. 1, 2.
[3] xviii. 18. xx. 16. xvi. 3. xxi. 24, compared with xiii. 39. xxi. 21.
[4] 1 Cor. xv. 12. cf. 2 Tim. ii. 18.

The difficulty may be met, perhaps, by saying that, as a system of doctrine, Christianity undoubtedly suffered both from Judaic formalism at home and from Judaic licence abroad, but that, as a moral progress, it owed its development neither to the extreme right nor to the extreme left of its leading exponents. The strength of the Church in its youth lay in its great central body of believers of all nationalities, uneducated, but unprejudiced; untrained, but not unprepared, for the liberty of the life in Christ. To explain this we must remind the reader that, although in the New Testament Jew and Gentile are sharply contrasted, yet as a matter of fact the gulf was bridged over by a series of gradations; and further that the gospel in contact with pure heathenism hardly comes into view at all. The first Christian Evangelists were Jews preaching to Jews, or to Gentiles already under Jewish influence. Indeed it has been contended that for a quarter of a century, at least, perhaps not a single convert was won over who was not to some extent acquainted with the religion or with the sacred writings of the Jews, and therefore to that extent prepared for the acceptance of the gospel. Certainly when this acquaintance was lacking the result was not encouraging. When S. Paul, the most venturesome of the band, addressed himself, against his will, to a purely heathen audience, he was not only not successful but he was scarcely even intelligible. As a "god" or as a "babbler" he was equally remote from his hearers.[1] But between strict Judaism and pure Paganism there were proselytes of the 'covenant' and of the 'gate,' circumcised and uncircumcised, and besides these a vast number of persons in Greek towns, Roman colonies, and in Rome itself, attracted to the Jews, but not committed to their faith, students of their literature and spectators of their rites.[2] Here lay the hope of Apostolic Christianity. Interested listeners fell into groups and united groups swelled into congregations. The Church at Philippi in the year 62 (?), the date of S. Paul's Epistle to the Philippians, furnishes, perhaps, as bright an example as can be found of a free, healthy and intelligent Christian community. Placed on the high-way between Europe and Asia, with only a small but sufficient Jewish population, enlightened by intercourse with two worlds, safe from circumcisers on the one hand and from philosophisers on the other, this Roman colony received and maintained to the time of the apostle's death a pure and simple faith. No doctrinal errors are laid to the charge of these trusty converts. Indeed it was not difficult for them to be orthodox. For the rule of their faith they had the Old Testament in its Greek version, including apocryphal and perhaps even pseudonymous

---

[1] Acts xiv. 18. xvii. 19.

[2] On the foreign settlements of the Jews and on the interest and respect which they excited, see Stanley, "*The Judaizers of the Apostolical Age*," with his references to Milman and Neander. See also Wellhausen on the Diaspora in his *History of Israel and Judah.*

books, and the 'Words of the Lord' in traditional
oral form ; whilst for the confession of their faith they
used a few simple articles of belief in Christ connected
with the leading facts, so far as they knew them, of
his life.[1] Knowledge of the One True God, trust in
His Son as the Saviour of the world, assurance of
pardon, hope of eternal life—these were the main
pillars of the truth which they held. Apart from the
special influence of the gospel-message and of its
boundless promise, the revelation of the One God,
served without altars and approached without a priest,
and the offer of rich and sacred Books to be henceforth
his own, must have had for the heathen learner weary
of profanity in religion and in literature a strong attraction. The study of prophecy and its application to the
secular as well as to the religious world would be full of
fascination. And, lastly, the sense of Christian brotherhood, and of membership in the Kingdom, must have
been sweet to those who cherished the memory of past
liberties and knew themselves to be the subjects, but
could never hope to be the citizens, of a jealous Empire.

[1] S. Paul's writings were apparently collected and circulated
before the middle of the second century, but they were not yet
regarded as a portion of Holy Writ and were therefore not
generally nor absolutely authoritative. If they are quoted by
the so-called Apostolic Fathers, it is not with the prefatory
ἡ γραφὴ λέγει, γέγραπται, &c., which mark citations from the Old
Testament. In fact for more than one hundred years S. Paul's
theology was intelligible only to a highly trained Jew. At the
same time the effect of his ethical and spiritual teaching was
doubtless wider and more immediate.

We must be careful, then, not to regard the primitive Christian religion as compounded from other systems. It had, as we have seen, a vital independent energy of its own, drawn from the land of its birth. But that it was affected by the cults, philosophies, and forms of government of the day, this of course cannot be denied. It was an age in religious matters at once credulous and cautious, attracted by novelty and yet intolerant of change. To forget the religion of his fathers was as impossible to the Gentile as to the Jew. We shall not be surprised, therefore, to see the new faith gathering into itself and preserving the customs of the Law[1] side by side with heathen usages; finding room for Jewish apocalypse, Greek theosophy, and Oriental mystery; and organising itself under forms of government partly ecclesiastical and partly civil. It is not for us to pronounce too positively to what extent Christianity clothed itself, as it went, in vesture not its own. All that we can honestly do is to gather into view certain cotemporary facts. Some of the resemblances may only be coincidences. We may mistake independent action

[1] The Law, it was soon felt, could not be maintained as a whole. At the same time it was admitted to be of divine origin. If the Mosaic system could be shown to have been typical, and therefore transitory, then the opposition of Law and Gospel would cease, and the two faiths would be welded into one. This is the line of argument pursued occasionally, but not always consistently, by S. Paul and, with stronger emphasis and more copious illustration, by the writer of the Epistle to the Hebrews. Little did either writer foresee the extent to which their method of syncretism would afterwards be applied.

for imitation, and justifiable compromise for corruption. We must therefore beware of hasty inference, and still more of hasty censure, remembering how difficult it is for any body at once to reform its own first mistakes, and that the very name of Reformation brings the reproach of error very near to our own times.

Hellenism is the term used for the Greek influence which began to flow into the East from the day when Alexander the Great crossed the Hellespont in the year B.C. 334. The spirit of the Greek race never really passed into Asia, for the energies and character of one people cannot pass to another, but with the march of the Macedonian phalanx began the movement which by the end of the next century had spread the language, the military organization, the methods of civil government, the social habits and, to a certain extent, the culture of Greece over Asia Minor, Syria, and Mesopotamia. What a world of change lies in a single passage like this, bound up in many an English Bible between the Old and New Testaments, unread and unknown ! " Jason the high priest built a gymnasium under the citadel itself and made the young men practise gymnastics, and the adoption of Greek fashion ran to such a height that the priests cared no longer to serve the altar but despised the temple and neglected the sacrifices and were eager to share in the forbidden entertainment of the palæstra which began

with a challenge to throw the quoit."[1]   This passage
marks almost the middle point between the death of
Alexander and the birth of Christ.   From David's
'citadel' the eye looks out on a strangely altered scene.
After two centuries of subjection to Persian rule the
Jews had for another hundred years paid tribute to the
Græco-Egyptian crown.   They were now tributaries of
the Græco-Syrian kings.   Lying between these rival
powers, the borders of their land had been crossed and
recrossed by chariots and elephants and horsemen,[2] as
the balance of victory inclined to the North or to the
South.   These borders had shrunk to narrower limits.
The Greek and Græcized towns of the West Coast
divided the people of Judæa and of Galilee from their
own sea.   On the Eastern side of the Jordan were the
more completely Hellenized towns of Gerasa and Philadelphia, Gadara and Pella, spreading not only the
manners of the Greeks, but also the legends and altars
of the gods of Greece.   Within the central district, in
Panias (Cæsarea Philippi), in Scythopolis, and in the
city of Samaria, Hellenism had gained a nearer footing.
And now in Jerusalem itself there was a strong
Hellenizing party eager to bear the names of Grecian
heroes, to wear the honours of Grecian athletes and to
be enrolled as citizens of heathen Antioch.   At
Alexandria there were as many Jews as Greeks.   In
that freer air, for the use of the Jewish colony, the
Hebrew Scriptures had for the most part been translated

[1] 2 Macc. iv. 12—14.   Cf. 1 Macc. i. 11—15.   [2] 1 Macc. i. 17.

H

into Greek with a freedom which did not hesitate to
vary, to soften, to supplement, or even to omit, portions
of the original text in order to adapt it to the compass
of a wider and more modern knowledge.[1] A glance
forward from this same midway point will shew us
stronger evidence of the growth of the Greek spirit. It
is true that when eight years later, by order of the
Syrian King, the altar of Jupiter has been placed upon
the altar of Jehovah, a strong national party under the
sons of Mattathias will fight to the death for the
religion of their fathers. It is true that one of these
leaders, Judas Maccabæus, will recover Jerusalem and
restore the worship of the temple, that others of the
same line will afterwards carry the success of Jewish
arms as far to the West as Joppa and as far to the East
as Gerasa, and not only destroy for a time some of the
strongholds of heathen worship but even force the
descendants of Ishmael in the North and of Esau in the
South to accept circumcision and the law of Moses.
But it must be borne in mind that the Maccabæan
revolt was not against Hellenism but heathenism, that
is to say, that it resisted Hellenic culture only in the
department of religious worship. The Hellenizing high
priest Alcimus was so well supported that he was able
to check and even for a time to triumph over the
followers of Judas. Judas himself does not hesitate to

---

[1] The collected translations were afterwards known as the
Septuagint when a mass of legend had gathered round the
translators and the scene of their labours.

send ambassadors to ask alliance with the rising power
of Rome. Jonathan his brother, half soldier and half
priest, adds to the high priest's turban a golden crown
received from the Syrian king. The last of the
brothers, Simon, receives by favour of the same foreign
power the title ' Prince of Judæa.' John Hyrcanus,
son of Simon, at the head of Jewish troops, finds no
difficulty in serving with Antiochus Sidetes in a distant
campaign against the king of Parthia. His sons are
known by Greek names, and the eldest, ' the
Philhellen,' styles himself the ' King of the Jews' and
wears, like the kings of the Greek Empire, a royal
diadem. Foreign mercenaries are paid with foreign
coin and the royal priesthood surrounds itself with
something of the state of a foreign court. At last the
sacerdotal functions have become so small a part of the
royal office that the reigning Sovereign, acting on a
foreign usage, nominates his successor and even a
woman ascends the throne (B.C. 79). And when,
fifteen years later, Pompey marches on Jerusalem, he
finds a strong faction more than ready to open the
gates, to help him to besiege the temple-heights and to
join with his soldiers in the massacre of the priests.
From this point the mind of the outer world writes
itself in deeper characters on the soil of Palestine. A
stronger hand than that of Egypt, stronger than that of
Syria, re-imposes tribute and brings the show of independence to an end. By order of a Roman proconsul
the Hellenistic towns of Palestine rise again from their

ruins and their altars smoke once more with heathen rites. A few years later Herod the Great, of doubtful birth and more than doubtful faith, will receive in Rome itself amidst idolatrous sacrifice the kingly title, will draw his body-guard from German and Celtic tribes, choose the companions of his leisure from Greek men of letters and make amongst the civilians of Judæa a new political party distinguished by his name. He will be ready with impartial zeal to repair Apollo's temple at Rhodes, to restore Jehovah's temple at Jerusalem, and to dedicate two temples in two Cæsareas to Augustus and to Rome. In connection with this new cult public games must be instituted in honour of the Emperor and repeated every fourth year. Before Herod's reign was over, Cæsarea on the coast and Jericho on the opposite side had a theatre for plays, an amphitheatre for the fights of wild beasts, a circus for the chariot race. To the same founder Jerusalem owed its theatre and amphitheatre, its stadium and hippodrome. The courts and colonnades of the temple were in the Grecian style. The constitutions of the country-towns were modelled after Greek examples. Inns and baths and markets threw into the severity of Jewish life the gaiety of the Western world. In fact the air of Palestine in the time of Christ was heavy with the breath of other lands. There was but one barrier between the native and the foreigner—the law of Levitical uncleanness—and, with the exception of certain forms of contact not easily purified, there was nothing to check the freest intercourse with the soldiers and sightseers, traders and travellers, who swarmed in every port and crowded every road. It would be as absurd to attempt to gather the condition of Palestine in that age from the reports of the Evangelists as it would be to try to write the history of our own times from the Reports of Convocation. Our authorities present only the religious aspect of certain selected incidents within a certain selected area. But we learn from other sources with startling certainty that the Pharisees and Sadducees of Jerusalem and the peasants of Galilee were not the only, or even the largest, groups upon the stage when Jesus of Nazareth crossed the scene.

Going back to the same starting-point, we see the effect of foreign influence throughout the same period in another department, that of literature. Fragments still preserved of a poem in Greek hexameters and of a tragedy in iambic trimeters, both written in the second century before Christ, and both setting forth in epic and dramatic form the matter of the sacred scriptures, show that the Hebrew mind even then was not insensible to the charm of Greek poetry. The language and the metre of Homer are used to recommend Jewish faith, and oracles in good round hexameters foretelling the fate of an impenitent world are placed in the mouth of the ancient Sibyl. Verses, forged and genuine, are given as quotations from Hesiod and Orpheus, from Æschylus and Sophocles, in order to inculcate a belief in the true God. Here, of course, it is only or chiefly the outward style which attracts the Jewish author. But before long the modes of Greek thought also will throw their spell upon his work. Extracts from the writings of Aristobulus who lived about the middle of the same century show an acquaintance with Greek philosophy and a desire to blend the teaching of Moses with that of Pythagoras and Plato. In the so-called 'Wisdom of Solomon' the influence of Aristotle is clearly traceable, whilst Wisdom is theorised into a distinct entity in passages which Plato might have written—an existence so real and life-like that it almost suggests the 'Persons' within the Godhead which Greek speculation afterwards developed within and without the realm of Christian theology.[1] The noblest fruit of Greek philosophy, the doctrine of a future life, is more conspicuous here than in any other Jewish writing, and its Greek origin is shown in this, that the author presents that life from the Socratic point of view as the immortality of the soul only, and not as a resurrection of the body.

But it is in the works of Philo of Alexandria, nearly cotemporary with Christ, that we find the richest and fullest results of the union of Western thought and Oriental belief. By birth and education a Jew, by

---

[1] "Some maintain that the Trinity of the Christians was but an imitation of that of the Alexandrians ; others accuse the Alexandrians of being the imitators. The dispute has been angrily conducted on both sides." Lewes, *History of Philosophy.*

study and mental habit a Greek, he illustrates in himself, as he proposes to others, the alliance of philosophy and religion. The Mosaic Legislation is his great theme. To the Jews it shall be still more precious, for he will show them how all along they had possessed in their Law, without knowing it, a philosophy ; from the Greek it shall receive respect, for he will make it clear that, before the rise of any system in Greece, Moses under inspiration had already taught in the wilderness the principles of all their Schools, that from him they were even derived. To fulfil this double aim he strains his sacred text to the breaking point in the vain attempt to find a common basis for processes so fundamentally different in their method as speculation and revelation. It was a fatal precedent. In the hands of Christian Fathers allegorical commentary and mystical interpretation afterwards extracted from the sober sense of Scripture types and prophecies, analogies and adumbrations, to the glory of theology and to the shame of true religion.[1]

[1] Let a few instances suffice by way of illustration. The twelve bells and the twelve gems of the high priest's robe, the twelve fountains of Elim and the twelve stones chosen by Joshua from Jordan, prefigured the twelve apostles. *Justin Martyr and Tertullian.*—The scarlet line of Josh. ii. 21 was symbolical of the redeeming blood of Christ. *Clement of Rome*— Moses' Ethiopian wife is a type of the Gentile Church. *Irenæus.* —Foreshadowings of the cross have been found in the wood for the burnt offering which Isaac carried, in the stick on which the scarlet wool was bound, and even in Jael's tent-peg.—The raising of the Shunammite's son indicates infant baptism, just as the bread and wine offered by Melchisedek are an intimation of the

The use of the pen in the diffusion of new ideas during the period of which we have been speaking is found chiefly amongst the Jews of the Dispersion. In Palestine the influx of fresh thought reached the people rather through the action of religious parties. The Pharisees, the ' Separated,' took their rise as the anti-Hellenizing party about a century and a-half before the birth of Christ; but, though they showed a conservative spirit in resisting the adoption of " Greek fashion," they either could not, or would not, oppose the introduction of foreign questions and speculations. That they had against them the Sadducees who adhered jealously to that which was revealed in the written law of Moses, is a proof that by some of their countrymen they were regarded as innovators. It was

Eucharist. *Clement of Alexandria and Cyprian.*—In the eyes of Justin and Tertullian the passage of the Red Sea and the offering of fine flour in the treatment of leprosy point the same way.—The words 'cave' and 'bread' in the Septuagint rendering of Is. xxxiii. 16 disclose the grotto of the Nativity and the very name of Bethlehem. *Justin.*—To the same writer " The government upon his shoulder " means the extension upon the cross; the two goats in Lev. xvi. 7, are the two Advents, and the number of persons saved in the ark is a symbol of the day on which Christ rose from the dead.—When the children mocked Elisha, they prefigured the Crucifixion; for they cried after him " *Go up, Calve!* " and Christ was mocked and *went up* to *Calvary*. *Augustine.*—On the continuance in early Christian exegesis of the allegoric temper of the Sophists and of the Stoical Schools in the interpretation of ancient Greek poetry, see Hatch, *Hibbert Lectures*, 1888, III., and, for a defence of the mystical interpretation of Scripture, Newman, *Development of Christian Doctrine*, vii. 4.

afterwards explained on their behalf, by the convenient fiction of "the oral law," that their tenets with regard to fate and free-will, their angelology, their doctrine of the intermediate state and of a future life—distinctly traceable to external sources—were not imported beliefs, but parts of an unwritten revelation derived from Moses himself. But the absence of all historical argument in favour of this position is in itself a sufficient answer to those who would defend it.

More deserving of attention is the constitution of that ascetic order which from the middle of the same century began to establish itself in special houses throughout Palestine and settled in greater numbers in the valley of the Jordan and by the shores of the Dead Sea. "The Essene," it has been said, "is the enigma of Hebrew history." He comes unobserved with a name unexplained, leaves no record of himself, and is passed over in silence by those who knew him best. From Philo and Josephus we learn that the Essenes were strictly organised, that they had a community of property, that they laboured only at honest and peaceful crafts, that they abstained from marriage and from oaths, that they condemned animal sacrifice and were therefore excluded from the temple, that they were strict sabbatarians, attached much importance to constant lustrations, turned towards the sun when praying, and held the doctrine of the passage of the soul to joy or woe when separated from the perishable prison of the flesh. As for the formation of Essenism, whilst some writers explain it by a Jewish foundation, with added elements derived from Parseeism and, perhaps, Buddhism, others account for all its peculiarities by referring them to Pythagorean influence.[1]

We have now with rough and rapid touch followed the several threads of foreign influence down to the point at which they meet in the Judaism of the Herodian age. It is Judaism with a difference. It is Mosaism

[1] Josephus suggests the latter conclusion, δίαιτῃ χρώμενον τῇ παρ᾽ Ἕλλησιν ὑπὸ Πυθαγόρου καταδεδειγμένῃ, Ant. xv. 10, 4, quoted by Lightfoot. Schürer, following Zeller, gives the subjoined parallels with Pythagoreanism—Lustrations, severe simplicity of life, scrupulous avoidance of everything unclean, white garments, exaltation of celibacy, the invocation of the sun, and, lastly, the dualistic doctrine of the relation of soul and body. But he allows that both systems may have drawn these peculiarities from one common Oriental source. This would throw us back again upon the Persian and Indian points of origin already mentioned. It is difficult to measure the intercourse between India and the West in the pre-Christian period dating from the conquests of Alexander, but there is sufficient evidence to make it as difficult to deny that it existed. See the authorities given in Lightfoot, *Colossians*, p. 390, and an article by M. Émile Burnouf in the *Revue des Deux Mondes*, July 15th, 1888, *Le Bouddhisme en Occident*. For further inquiry the following references may be useful :—*Buddhism in Christianity*, A. Lillie, 1887. *Buddhism*, Hibbert Lectures, 1881. *Das Evangelium von Jesu in seinen Verhältnissen zur Buddha-sage*, Seydel, 1882. *Die Buddha-Legende und das Leben Jesu*, Seydel, 1884. *Buddhism*, The Church Quarterly Review, Oct., 1890. *Buddhism in the New Testament*, The Arena, April, 1891. *Christianity and Buddhism* (Prof. Max Müller), The New Review, Jan., 1891. See also the Article *Gnosticism*, Encyclop. Britannic., and, for adverse criticism on Seydel's conclusions, Prof. Chantepie de la Saussaye, *Lehrbuch der Religionsgeschichte*.

still, but Mosaism modified by contact with many masters. A captive and an exile abroad, a vassal at home; blocked from without and garrisoned within; washed by every wave of conquest, and feeling every change of hand, from Persian satrap down to Roman procurator; placed on the very line where the currents from the East and from the West met and crossed; living amid the sights and sounds of foreign life and learning through alien tongues the thoughts of alien minds; a Hebrew in Jerusalem and a Hellenist in Alexandria; it would have been strange indeed if, after the Return, the Jew had remained for five hundred years what he had been under his own monarchy. The change was not altogether on the side of gain. If he gathered from the East a nobler conception of God and a more spiritual worship, he gathered also those lower suggestions which added the magic of Babylon to the magic of Egypt,[1] developed the orders of angels and of devils,

[1] For the prevalence of belief in magic down to the time of the Captivity, see the able and liberal article *Urim and Thummim* in Smith's *Dictionary of the Bible*, with the works there cited, and, for an account of magic among the Chaldæans, Lenormant's exhaustive work, and, for the testimony of Scripture generally, consult the following passages:—Gen. xxxi. 30, 32. xliv. 5. Exod. vii. 8—12, 22. viii. 7. Deut. xviii. 9—14. Num. xxiii. 23. Josh. xxiv. 10. Judges xvii. 5. xviii. 4, 5. 1 Sam. xv. 23. xxviii. 3—20. 2 Kings xxiii. 24. 2 Chron. xxxiii. 6. Ezra xxi. 21. Is. ii. 6. xiii. 19. xix. 3. xxix. 3, 4. xlvii. 12, 13. Jer. xiv. 14. xxiii. 25. xxvii. 9, 10. xxix. 8, 9. Ezek. xiii. 17, 23. xxi. 21. Hos. iii. 4, 5. Micah iii. 6, 7, 11. v. 12. Zech. x. 2. Tobit vi. 7. viii. 2, 3. Matt. xii. 27. Acts viii. 9, 11. xiii. 6. xix. 19. Gal. v. 20. 2 Thess. ii. 9. Rev. ix. 21. xiii. 13—15. xvi. 14. xix. 20. xxi. 8.

invented the follies of the Haggada, and heaped the pains of Gehenna on the terrors of the grave. If from the West came philosophy, with philosophy came the double tendency to turn religion from the healthy play of righteous conduct into the science of the school, or the discipline of the cell ; thus producing the Pharisee and the Essene, or, in other words, the theologian and the monk. And the point to which our argument is bringing us is this, that, as at the dawn of the Christian era there was no fixed type of Judaism and as little union between the synagogues of the Dispersion as between the sects of Palestine, so it would be unreasonable to suppose that in the next age Christianity, itself a product of Judaism, would exhibit any stability or uniformity as a whole. To show how the influences which penetrated the earlier system operated even more powerfully on the later will be the object of the next chapter.

CHAPTER VI

The Kingdom and the World.

PART II.

There was this difference detween Greek and Jewish philosophy,[1] that the former disengaged itself from religious tradition, whilst the latter could do nothing without it. The first advanced by a series of independent speculations, the second by a process of determined interpretations. The Greek solved new problems by inventing new theories, the Jew by applying old authorities. On the one hand we have the fresh conclusions of scientific study, on the other the scientific study of past conclusions. When the canon of Scripture was closed, the work of the Scribe began. Out of the legal elements of the written code he elaborated in fullest detail a body of unwritten law; out of the historical portions he developed a mass of explanatory narrative and edifying legend. He did this at first in perfect good faith. "*Fingunt simul creduntque.*" He brought forth out of his treasure, as he believed, things new and old, the new already existing by implication in the

[1] Philo, in the *Vita Mosis*, speaks of the '$\pi\acute{a}\tau\rho\iota o\nu$ $\phi\iota\lambda o\sigma o\phi\acute{\iota}a\nu$' studied in the synagogues of Palestine.

old. Whether the fresh matter were educed by logical deduction, or by allegorical interpretation, or by pure manipulation, was of no consequence. It was not the end only that justified the means. The sacred text came from a divine source, and, under religious handling, could yield no sense that would not also be divine. Meaning of some sort could always be forced from any sentence, if only by transposing the order of the words, or by pressing the numerical value of the letters. It was a childish game, notwithstanding the gravity of the players. But the point to be noted here is the fact that the Jewish methods of exegesis—if exegesis it can be called—flowed on without check or change into Christian interpretation. Indeed there was never more than one stream, for, though the Christian Church included Gentile converts, its literature was shaped by Jewish hands. S. Paul may have attended lectures in heathen philosophy at Tarsus—he shows some acquaintance with heathen poets—and his master Gamaliel is said to have allowed the study of heathen literature. But the principles of the Jewish schools took deepest root. It was impossible for him to unlearn and to disuse the mysteries of the craft to which he had been trained.[1] When he says that the Israelites drank of a rock that followed them,[2] he gives a different turn to a Rabbinical legend which he neither accepts literally nor denies absolutely; when he says in the next chapter[3]

---

[1] See Acts xxii. 3. Gal. i. 14. Phil. iii. 5, 6.   [2] 1 Cor. x. 4.
[3] 1 Cor. xi. 10. Cf. Jude 6.

that a woman ought to have a sign of authority on her
head, because of the angels, he takes quite seriously the
Rabbinical interpretation of Gen. vi. 2, and regards as
a serious danger the exposure of the unveiled head to
the prying gaze of invisible beings. In a famous
passage[1] he ventures on an allegorical experiment of his
own and, by a forced and intricate analogy, draws from
the life of Abraham and from the geographical position
of Mount Sinai a prefigurement of the rise and triumph
of the Christian Church.[2] But the heavenly Jerusalem
and the persecuting insolence of Ishmael are touches
thrown in from existing traditions. It is on similar
authority that he rests when he says that the law was
"ordained through angels,"[3] that at the raising of the
dead "the trumpet shall sound,"[4] that he had been
"caught up to the *third* heaven."[5] By a similar sanction he would have defended the grammatical quibble
which proves the promised descent of Christ from
Abraham,[6] and the quotation of passages from the
prophets wrested from their original application and
adduced as arguments in favour of Justification by
Faith,[7] or in depreciation of the Gift of Tongues.[8] If

---

[1] Gal. iv. 22—31.

[2] The words συστοιχεῖ and ἀλληγορούμενα suggest reminiscences
of the lecture-room. See Lightfoot *ad loc.*

[3] Gal. iii. 19. Cf. Heb. ii. 2.   [4] 1 Cor. xv. 52.   [5] 2 Cor. xii. 2.

[6] Gal. iii. 16.   See also 1 Cor. ix. 8—10; 2 Cor. iii. 7, 13.

[7] Gal. iii. 11.   Rom. i. 17.   (Hab. ii. 4).

[8] 1 Cor. xiv. 21.   (Is. xxviii. 11).   The argument of Rom.
ix. x. xi. may be taken as an example of S. Paul's method of
Scriptural proof.

he wrote the Epistles to the Ephesians and to the Colossians, in these he presents in ascending and descending scale the orders of angels good and evil under the names by which they were known in the speculations of the schools.[1] Some would claim for him the reference to the legend in which the names of Pharaoh's magicians were preserved.[2] Nor does he stand alone amongst the writers of the New Testament in his acquaintance with the "traditions of the elders." One author[3] tells us that Michael the archangel contended with Satan for the body of Moses; from another[4] we learn that the great drought of 1 Kings xvii. 1, continued, not at the word, but at the prayer of Elijah, and, not for three years, but for three years and six months. But we may pass on to note how, true to the methods in which they had been schooled, all these writers find symbols and intimations ready to their hand in authorised Scripture as well. The ancient texts lent themselves as easily to Christian as to Jewish interpretation. The rival faiths feathered their arrows with the same arguments. There was no event or character in Old Testament history, no rite or ordinance, sacred act or sacred object, which could not in the skilled hands of such expounders serve as types

---

[1] Eph. i. 21. ii. 2. vi. 12. Col. i. 16. ii. 10, 15.

[2] 2 Tim. iii. 8.

[3] Jude 9. For other instances in this Epistle of reference to legendary matter, see verses 5 (with reading 'Jesus' for 'Lord') 11, and 14.

[4] Jas. v. 17.

and predictions of the new dispensation.[1] Resemblances are seized, not as illustrations, but as arguments, not as accidental similitudes, but as ordained examples, and in many cases it is really the supposed type which suggests the antitype, and the passing shadows of the Law throw further and fuller shadows of good things to come. This study of correspondences is especially observable in the Epistle to the Hebrews. The writer grasps the mysterious figure of the Canaanite Melchizedek as he crosses the path of Abraham for a moment, and does not release it until it has testified to the nature, office, and rank of Christ and to the abolition of the Levitical priesthood.[2] Abel[3] forebodes the death of Christ, and Isaac[4] his resurrection. The Tabernacle and its ritual, its altars and its sacrifices, even its plan and its furniture,[5] are divine patterns which have their counterparts in the constitution of the Christian Church.[6] In fact Judaism is to give its impress to

[1] "All things are double one against another"—Ecclus. xlii. 24.

[2] Heb. vii. 1—22. The argument that the kingly priesthood of Christ was foreshewn in Melchizedek is a little marred by the probability that Melchizedek was priest of an idolatrous worship and was not, in the ordinary sense of the term, a king at all. 'Salem' appears to have been a local name for a Babylonian divinity, the god of the rising sun. See Prof. Sayce on ' *Melchizedek, king of Salem.*'

[3] xii. 24.   [4] xi. 17. 19.   [5] ix. x. 1—22.

[6] For other forced applications in this Epistle of the primary sense and intention of words and names dissociated from their context, see i. 5, 6, 8—12, 13. ii. 7, 12, 13. iv. 7, 8. v. 10. vii. 3, 6, 8, 9. ix. 16. The Epistle to the Hebrews is Alexandrian

I

Christianity and then the seal is to be broken. Can we wonder that the Jews of a later age cursed the Christians in their daily prayers?[1]   It must have been difficult to forgive, not so much their disobedience to the Law, as their justification of that disobedience by the very language of the Law. Yet from their own fathers had come the secret of mystical exposition which was now turned against them. The climax of this false exegesis was reached, perhaps, when an honoured 'Apostolic Father' found the form of the Saviour's Cross and the first two letters of his name in the number of the men whom Abraham circumcised in his household.[2]   But the method itself lived on. It passed from Apostle to Father and from Father to Schoolman and there are some even now to whom it is as convincing as it is attractive. The three senses of Scripture maintained by Swedenborg and his " science of correspondences" show the length to which it has been carried in modern times.

from beginning to end and leads the way in the Christian use of the allegorical method of interpretation which was afterwards associated with the Catechetical School of Alexandria and found its chief exponents in Pantænus, Clement, and Origen.

[1] Justin, Dial. c. Tryph. 16, 47, 93, 96, 108, 117, 137 ; Jerome, *Commentarii in Iesaiam* (ed. Vallarsi) 81, 565, 604.

[2] *Epistle of Barnabas*, ix.—300=I H; 18=T; cf. Gen. xiv.14. To remove all doubt as to his own conviction, he adds that he had never taught a more certain truth. A comparison of the exposition by Philo of the symbolism of the Tabernacle and its furniture with that of Josephus will shew the licence and extravagance of the method and the variety of its results.

Another factor in the formation of early Christian doctrine is the influence of apocalyptic writings. These compositions by unknown authors take their rise in the second century before Christ and run on through the first century of our era. Some, as the Book of Daniel and the Book of Enoch, are purely Jewish; others, as the Testaments of the Twelve Patriarchs, appear to be Jewish originals interpolated by Christian hands. All have the same object, to comfort and to encourage a depressed people by visions of future glory and greatness veiled in enigmatic form and certified by the stamp of some great historic name. The writers are not anonymous, but pseudonymous, though their frauds are not less pious than some which have found excuse. Their influence on the popular mind and on later literature cannot be questioned. The Book of Enoch is directly quoted in the Epistle of Jude and references may be discovered in the Book of the Revelation. It is the *Inferno* of Jewish literature and to this, more than to any other source, may be traced the passages in the New Testament which speak of the doom of angels and of men, the final judgment of the wicked and the punishing fires of hell.

Closely connected with mystical interpretation and apocalyptic vision is the revival, with a difference, of the prophetic office in the Christian congregation. The writer of the Revelation claims for himself the title of prophet,[1] and for his book the character of prophecy.[2]

---

[1] Rev. xxii. 9. [2] xxii. 7.

Prophets are classed by him with saints and apostles.[1]
Prophets come down from Jerusalem to the church at
Antioch ;[2] they give their name to local ministers in
the same church ;[3] and they rank next to the Apostles
in the Church at large.[4] Power might come to them
with or without the laying on of hands.[5] The fact of
martyrdom for Christ was sufficient proof of the spirit
of prophecy in the martyr.[6] Even the confession of
Jesus as Lord was a result of prophetic inspiration.[7]
When S. Paul speaks of visions and revelations and
unspeakable words, he would have it understood that he
also had passed through the prophetic trance.[8] Prophecy
he regards as a distinct manifestation of the Spirit.[9]
A revelation might be made at any moment to any
member, whether within or without the official body.[10]
Even women could possess the gift.[11] With the grace
of supernatural illumination[12] was sometimes bestowed
the power of predicting future events,[13] or of signifying

[1] xvi. 6. xviii. 20.   [2] Acts xi. 27.   [3] Acts xv. 32, Cf. xiii. 1.
[4] 1 Cor. xii. 28. Eph. ii. 20. iii. 5. iv. 11. Cf. the language
of the *Te Deum* (vv. 7, 8) and the Collect for SS. Simon and
Jude in our Prayer-book. See also Matt. x. 41. xxiii. 34. vii.
22. xxiv. 11, 24.
[5] Acts viii. 17. vi. 10. xix. 6. x. 44—46. xi. 15. 1 Cor. xiv. 1, 5, 39.
[6] Rev. xix. 10.   [7] 1 Cor. xii. 3. 1 John iv. 1—3.
[8] 2 Cor. xii. 1, 4, 7. 1 Cor. xiii. 2. xiv. 6. Gal. i. 12.
[9] Rom. xii. 6. 1 Cor. xii. 10, 29. xi. 5. Gal. iii. 5. Cf. 2 Pet.
i. 21. 1 Thess. v. 20.
[10] 1 Cor. xiv. 26, 30.   [11] Acts xxi. 9.
[12] 1 Cor. ii. 10—16. vii. 40. 1 John ii. 20.
[13] Acts xi. 28. xx. 23. xxi. 10. 1 Cor. ii. 10. xiii. 9. 1 Thess.
v. 2. 2 Thess. ii. 2. 1 Tim. iv. 1.

the right course of future action.[1]   The voice of the
prophet is the voice of the Holy Ghost, to prompt or
to prevent.[2]   The 'word of prophecy' had become
increasingly 'sure' and burned with steadier light.[3]
The 'faithful sayings' of the Pastoral Epistles are
possibly utterances of a similar nature.[4] Upon this
revival of prophetic fervour the passages cited in Peter's
first sermon from the Book of Joel throw abundant
light.[5] Was it not promised that the spirit should be
poured forth on *all* flesh, that young men should see
visions and old men dream dreams, that sons and
daughters, bondmen and bondmaidens, should prophesy?
But, though we may explain the origin, it is not easy
to measure the effects, of this ecstatic wave.   Its power
in shaping and colouring the narratives and speeches,
hopes and beliefs, of the New Testament is incalculable.
Prophecy was the golden key which unlocked the secrets
of all time.   It was a key which a child might turn.
No wonder if every one had "a psalm, a teaching, a
revelation, a tongue, an interpretation."[6]   There was
scarcely a sentence of ancient Scripture which was not
a prediction, and there was not a prediction which had

---

[1] Acts xvi. 6, 7, 10.

[2] Acts xiii. 2. xx. 28. 1 Tim. iv. 14.   Perhaps also Acts
iv. 31, 1 Cor. xiv. 36, Eph. vi. 17, 1 Tim. iv. 5, Heb. iv. 12, and
other passages in which 'the word of God' is used rather of
inward energy than of outward expression.   Even for Christians
of his own time (καὶ μέχρι νῦν) Justin claims the gift of prophecy;
Dial. c. Tryph.   [3] 2 Pet. i. 19. 1 Pet. i. 10, 11.

[4] 1 Tim. i. 15, iv. 9. 2 Tim. ii. 11. Tit. iii. 8.

[5] Acts ii. 7—21.   [6] 1 Cor. xiv. 26. Cf. Acts i. 15. ii. 1, 4.

not already fulfilled itself in the life of Christ or would not hereafter fulfil itself in the life of his Church. History might be written and theology might be taught by anyone who could read between the lines of prophecy.[1] Isaiah is cited between sixty and seventy times in the New Testament, the Psalms not less than seventy times; there are citations from eleven other prophets, Jeremiah, Daniel, Hosea, Joel, Amos, Jonah, Micah, Habakkuk, Haggai, Zechariah, Malachi; in The Revelation there is hardly a vision or symbol, metaphor or title, which is not borrowed from Ezekiel and other Old Testament prophets. Thus we see Christian thought rolling itself back on Jewish phraseology, to emerge afterwards as a new ecclesiastical system. "According to the Scriptures" is the certifying phrase which justifies every dogmatic statement and, in many cases, reveals the source.[2] The

---

[1] See 1 Cor. ix. 9. x. 11. Rom. xv. 4.

[2] The growth of the Judas legend is a good example of the growth of later narrative out of reflection upon ancient scripture. Whether there was any historical incident on which the story of the betrayal was founded we cannot now certainly say, but to read the ninth verse of the forty-first Psalm (cf. John xiii. 18) is to see the material ready laid for the construction of the words and acts recorded by the Evangelists in connection with the exposure and denunciation of the traitor at the Last Supper. If we accept the record as it stands, we find it difficult to explain the action of the Master, the attitude of the faithful disciples and the conduct of the traitor himself in that closing scene. (See Appendix II.) The difficulty is not diminished when we attempt to reconcile Matt. xxvii. 5 with Acts i. 18. The discrepancy between the two traditions is due to the fact that the

process of after-thought is naively confessed by the writer of the Fourth Gospel in ii. 22 (cf: xx. 9) refer- ring, it is supposed, to Ps. xvi. 10, and in xii. 16. With the same frankness Tertullian (Apol. xx.) says, " Hence it is that we come to be so infallibly certain of

former is more under the influence of the passage from Zechariah (xi. 12, 13) cited in evidence in Matt. xxvii. 9, 10. The etymology of the words Iscariot (' strangling') and Aceldama (' field of blood') helps the development of the legend—although here too there is a double tradition in consequence of two separate explanations of the 'blood' as the .Saviour's or the traitor's—and it finds its last touches in two more passages from the Psalms (lxix. 25. cix. 8) cited in Acts i. 20. As bearing upon the whole subject, the question might, perhaps, be raised whether S. Paul, when he says (1 Cor. xv. 5) that Christ after his resurrection appeared "to the twelve," does not literally mean to the twelve. It is easy to say that *The Twelve* was a name, not of number, but of office, but the appearance to which he refers is assumed to be the appearance to "the Eleven" in Matt. xxviii. 16, where the distinction as to number is carefully made. If *The Twelve* had a secondary and purely official sense, without regard to number, in the time of S. Paul, much more must that meaning have been fixed at the date of the First Gospel. Why does not the Evangelist use the same conventional expression? It is as difficult, however, to speak positively on one side as on the other. In 1 Cor. xi. 23 "betrayed" is nothing more than " delivered up," as in Rom. iv. 25.

As with the legend of Judas, so with the legends of the birth of Jesus, admission into the Canonical Gospels seems to have turned upon their correspondence to the ' prophecies' which they 'fulfil.' The Adoration of the Magi and the Flight into Egypt are in themselves not less improbable than many of the stories related in the apocryphal Gospels of the Infancy, but they have their parallels in the language of Psalmist and Prophet and are therefore " according to the Scriptures." For further instances see Appendix I.

many things which have not yet happened, from the experience that we have of those which are come to pass." " We know in part," says S. Paul, and, with equal candour he adds, " we prophesy (expound) in part."

This tendency to revert to the past and to re-absorb the institutions of the older faith finds another striking illustration in the rise of the Christian Ministry. There was at first no pressing necessity for the appointment of special officers. Each congregation was practically a synagogue and, unlike that of the temple, the system of the synagogue was purely congregational.[1] There was no appointed ' minister ' in the stricter sense of the word. Almost every member was qualified, and might be called upon to read, to expound, to instruct, to exhort. The Apostles, we know, were not church-officers. They were founders and fathers of churches, correspondents and referees, but they were not locally connected with any one church or group of churches. The name, it is true, was extended to other missionary preachers,[2] whilst the original body was distinguished as ' The Twelve ;'[3] but when the local churches were more numerous and more completely organized, then,

---

[1] For the Christian use of the term synagogue, see Jas. ii. 2, and for instances of action taken by the congregation as a whole, Acts i. 23. vi. 5. xi. 1—4, 22. xv. 12. xxi. 22. 2 Cor. ii. 6.

[2] Rom. xvi. 7. 1 Cor. iv. 6, 9. ix. 5. xv. 7. Gal. i. 1, 19. 1 Thess. ii. 6. Cf. 2 Cor. xi. 12—15.

[3] 1 Cor. xv. 5. Rev. xxi. 14. In two places S. Paul speaks of ' The Pre-eminent Apostles,' 2 Cor. xi. 5. xii. 11.

with the need, the title also of the ' missionary ' passed
away.[1]   Meanwhile, for the purposes of government, the
direction of affairs was entrusted more and more to
acknowledged leaders who formed a council of manage-
ment.   These officers were known in the Jewish-
Christian congregation, as in the Jewish synagogue, as
Elders, or Presbyters, and in Gentile communities by
the equivalent title of Episcopi, or Inspectors.   The
function of teaching was not necessarily part of their
office, but might be combined with it.[2]   By degrees the
term Episcopus attached itself to the leading Presbyter
within a certain area, and in the second century came to
be associated with the dignity and function of apostle-
ship.   A century later every Presbyter had become a
Priest and, with the revival of the principle of continual
propitiation deeply rooted both in Judaism and in
Paganism, the lay officer of the Christian synagogue
had been invested with the title and with the privileges
of the sons of Aaron.[3]   Upon this wilful retrogression

---

[1] See, however, "The Teaching of the Twelve Apostles" (A.D.
100 ?) Πᾶς δὲ ἀπόστολος ἐρχομενὸς πρός ὑμᾶς δεχθήτω 'ως Κυρίος. xi. 4.
But the 'prophet' holds a more prominent position and is more
frequently mentioned.   A little later and this title also dies
away, and prophetic utterance, as tending to discord in the
Churches, is expressly condemned.

[2] 1 Tim. v. 17.   It has been observed that the Pastoral Epistles
dwell very slightly on the office of teaching and do not even
mention the sacraments.

[3] The language of the earlier hierarchy was extended also to the
Deacons who were spoken of as Levites, though the precursor of
the deacon was probably the 'almoner' of the synagogue.

are based the doctrines of Apostolic and Sacerdotal Successions. It is difficult to argue with those who hold them still. " Christ instituted in his Church a permanent and official apostolate" says the latest priestly advocate.[1] " It is not to the apostle that we must look for the prototype of the bishop," said the most learned of modern bishops.[2] " The individual life can receive fellowship with God only by dependence upon social sacraments of regeneration, of confirmation, of communion, of absolution, of which ordained ministers are the appointed instruments," says the young theologian. " The Kingdom of Christ has no sacerdotal system," are the pondered words of the historian. The next age will wonder that this latter statement so easily proved was ever so seriously made, and still more that it was

---

[1] C. Gore, *The Church and the Ministry*, 1888.

[2] Lightfoot, *The Christian Ministry*, 1869. In the Didachè, or " Teaching of the Twelve Apostles " referred to above, the Bishop is the Successor rather of the 'Prophet' than of the Apostle,—λειτουργοῦρσι κὰι αὐτοὶ (ἐπίσκοποι καὶ διάκονοι) τὴν λειτουργίαν τῶν προφητῶν κὰι διδασκάλων, xv. 1. He is to be " elected" by the congregation and not to be "despised." See further Lefroy, *The Christian Ministry*, p. 413.—"The ἐπίσκοπος of the ancient Churches," says Dean Alford, " co-existed with, and did not in any sense succeed, the Apostles; and when it is claimed of bishops or any Church officers that they are their successors, it can be understood only chronologically, and not officially." Similarly Dean Plumptre :—" There is no trace of an order in the new Christian society, bearing the name, and exercising functions like those of the older Covenant. The idea which pervades the teaching of the Epistles is that of a universal priesthood."

ever disputed. At the same time it would be more accurate, perhaps, to say that the Kingdom of Christ had at first no sacerdotal system because, whilst the temple was standing, the thought of a separate system did not even present itself; that afterwards relapse into sacerdotalism, a creeping back into the warm shell of externalism, was almost unavoidable when religion was too young and too weak to emerge at once into spiritual independence; and that now in the foremost Churches of Christendom, even if Christianity had begun with a sacerdotal system, nothing would secure its continuance, nothing would prevent the very title of priest in its sacerdotal sense from becoming more and more a disused and derided name. The spirit of the reformed churches is a passion for justice, for enlightenment, for improvement. Not the pardon, but the prevention, of evil is their first aim. For the clergy as preachers and examples of righteousness there is place and power in the crowd, but the crowd will never again flock to them for the intercessions and absolutions of the sanctuary. The prophet's presentation of the earliest example of true priesthood furnishes the right model for these later days; " The law of truth was in his mouth, and unrighteousness was not found in his lips : he walked with me in peace and uprightnesss, and did turn many away from iniquity;"[1] and there is a touch of the same thought in the words of a modern seer; "He is the Prophet shorn of his more awful splendour; burning

[1] Mal. ii. 6.

with mild equable radiance, as the enlightener of daily life. This, I say, is the ideal of a Priest."[1] The love of sacred pomp lingers on in a nation long after the awe and fervour of the old worship have fled. The religious dread out of which ceremonials spring is followed by a superstitious dread of their omission. Then, in a later stage, reverence itself is lost, but the fondness for solemn spectacle remains, so that to most Englishmen a procession of priests on the stage is as moving and as real as a procession in a church. It is a perplexing sign when thoughtless folk, " the children in the markets," play with the solemnities of religion. In the old world, long after faith in the gods had died, victims bled and altars smoked to give a flavour of worship to the diversions of the crowd. Worship in its birth is a generous spiritual energy, but, when it is thrown out into form and sound, by a dangerous rebound it plays back upon the senses, becomes sensuous, till the worshipper is affected by the beauty of his own gifts, by the music of his own song, and is now a minister to his own delight.[2] It is always therefore a temptation to the multitude to dally with ceremonial, to run here and there as spectators and listeners, to love things sacred for their quaintness or their pathos, to insist at set times on

[1] Carlyle, *Heroes and Hero-Worship.*

[2] " I do not know, as I have repeatedly stated, how far the splendour of architecture, or other art, is compatible with the honesty and the usefulness of religious service. The longer I live the more I incline to severe judgment in this matter and the less I can trust the sentiments excited by painted glass and coloured tiles."—Ruskin, *Appendix to ' The Stones of Venice.'*

religious observances, not because religion prompts, but because custom demands. It is a perplexing sign, we say, when symbols of faith become toys of fashion, and the messages of heaven, to find the popular ear, must be dissolved into popular tunes.[1] Then is the time for the Puritan to speak, for some Moses to check the play in the camp by dashing the tables of stone amongst the gods of gold. He is the true priest who comes as from the mount of God, with the gravity of one who has communed with God, to tell the people that divine service is not a measured frolic, but an earnest subjection to divine laws ; that " God is spirit : and they that worship him must worship in spirit and truth ;" that therein is the Father glorified, " *that they bear much fruit.*"

Another determining influence which must not be overlooked is the ascetic tendency. This, as we have seen, made itself felt in Palestine in the form of Essenism, and Essenism we were inclined to refer to the action of foreign philosophic sects. When the Essene maintained that the flesh was the prison-house of the soul, he used the language of the later Pythagorean school. The teaching of the Cynics aimed at the

[1] " The concert was practically the only attraction of the day (Good Friday), but sufficed to bring to the Crystal Palace no fewer than 27,375 visitors. Mr. —— sang "Is it enough ?" with much power and feeling, and he was succeeded by Madame ——, whose " O, rest in the Lord" drew forth a storm of approbation which could only be allayed by her reappearance." *Daily Paper.*

subjugation of all natural desire, and the Stoics presented the same doctrine in a purified form. That matter is impure, that the human body is therefore the seat of the mind's impurity, is part of the system of Philo adapted from Plato. We may expect therefore to find traces of these current beliefs in the New Testament writers. It is part of the Pauline theology that through the trespass of the one the many died,[1] that sin is inherent in the flesh,[2] that in the flesh dwelleth no good thing.[3] These passionate statements must not be confused with the hard systems and theories of sin which have been developed from them, but they testify to the early working of that baneful pessimism which found expression in the austerities of Manichæan and Monastic discipline and still lurks in the folds of orthodox theology. The view of marriage in the New Testament is generally healthy and natural,[4] but there are indications[5] of the rise of that spirit which afterwards exalted the unwedded state, inspired and admired the monk and the nun and the celibate priest, and, even amongst ourselves, lingers on unsuspectedly in those who, refusing all evidence, maintain the perpetual virginity of the mother of Jesus.[6]

[1] Rom. v. 15.   [2] Rom. viii. 4—13.   Gal. v. 17.   1 Cor. xv. 50.
[3] Rom. vi. 6. vii. 18.
[4] Eph. v. 23—33.   1 Cor. vii. 5.   1 Tim. ii. 15. iv. 3. v. 14. Heb. xiii. 4.   1 Pet. ii. 7.
[5] Matt. xix. 12.   1 Cor. vii. 1, 7, 32, 34.   1 Tim. v. 11.   Rev. xiv. 4.
[6] For the evidence see Archdeacon Farrar on "The Lord's

Thus far we allow ourselves to trace the effects of foreign influence on the formation of Christian belief. The later grafts and inoculations are an interesting and fruitful study, but to account for them is not to account for the earlier stock which received and adopted them.

> " Nec longum tempus, et ingens
> Exiit ad cœlum ramis felicibus arbos,
> Miraturque novas frondes et non sua poma."

It is on the very root and origin of the Christian system that we are now intent. No ingenious theory of ' development' will satisfy us here. We have seen how the Jewish mind, distinguished from the first by its strong ethical bent, was set upon a law of righteous conduct, lost it, or forgot it, for a time in legal observance, and recovered it on a higher plane in the liberty of the Gospel; how Greek philosophy, on the other hand, starting from scientific speculation, turned more and more towards moral reformation, and, moving away from the old mythology, became, partly through the Greek translation of the Hebrew Scripture, increasingly conscious of the One God; how Christianity, springing from Jewish soil into a Greek atmosphere, satisfied both these movements, supplied the moral ideal and the right theological conception, and drew to itself the best efforts of Eastern and Western thought.

Brother " in *Smith's Dictionary of the Bible* and *Early Days of Christianity*, ch. xix. On the other side see Bp. Lightfoot, *Epistle to Galatians*, 247—282.

In the religion of Christ Hebrew and Heathen met rather by easy confluence than in conscious alliance, " in one Spirit baptized into one body whether Jews or Greeks, whether bond or free." The happiest results marked the first years of union. The wise and the mighty and the noble had not yet been called. There was no desire for metaphysical distinctions, for party conclusions sanctioned by the Church as dogmas and enforced by the State as decrees; rites and legends drawn from the mysteries and traditions of other cults had not yet filtered in to swell and darken the simple usages of Christian worship and the simple expressions of Christian faith; nor had ascetic fervour burnt its sickly brand too deeply into human bodies and the pleasures of human life. Gibbon in a famous chapter accounts for the spread of Christianity mainly by its doctrine of a future life, by the purity and austerity of its morals, by the union and discipline of its republic. But the hope of immortality, severe purity of life, and loyal fellowship were not unknown to the Religious Mysteries, Philosophic Schools, and Social Confraternities of the heathen world. The deeper causes lay in the offer to the Jew of a freer service, to the Gentile of a purer and more certain faith. Religion had never before been so open, so joyous, so sublime. Father, Son, Brethren, these were the living, loving words which sprang far a-head of all old-world speculation and worship and endeavour, and revealed as in a moment of time the right and true relation of God to

man, and of man to God, and of man to man. The
" great voices in heaven"[1] were really the cry of many
on earth, " The kingdom of the world is become the
kingdom of our Lord, and of his Christ."

[1] Rev. xi. 15.

" The Christian Creed cannot stop short of a social realisation. It deals with men, not as isolated units, but as members of a commonwealth."—*Westcott.*

" The only thing to regenerate the world is not more of any system, good or bad, but simply more of the Spirit of God."—*Kingsley.*

" He who shall introduce into public affairs the principles of primitive Christianity will revolutionise the world."—*Franklin.*

" By Freedom he meant the complete healthy development of their own natures, not a change of political institutions."—*Lewes*, Life of Goethe.

" Les principes de la religion peuvent seuls guérir les maladies qui travaillent le corps social."—*Balzac.*

CHAPTER VII.

The Kingdom and the Church.

The Kingdom, then, is Society under a new inspiration working out a new order. Because of the inspiration we may speak of the Church, and because of the order we may speak of the State, but to oppose one idea to the other is to oppose body and soul. "The kingdom of God is within you" is as true of the nation as of the man.

"The Church," it has been well said, "has only failed as civil society itself has failed." It could not be otherwise. They rise and fall together, for they are fused in one. Armies and police, prisons and work-houses, vice and crime, the tyranny of wealth, the servitude of want, if they mark the frustration of divine decree, mark no less the defeat of human government. The martial and the feudal and the sensual instincts in man have blocked his own path to better things. But, like the world on which he stands, he moves. The spirit of Christianity is the law which guides his course. It has infused itself into his domestic and social life, his art, his literature, his legislation, his politics at home, his policy abroad.

K 2

History adds its testimony day by day. The record of the last century is a record of increasing tenderness and sympathy and beneficence. The flowing tide of compassion has reached the slave and the prisoner, the ill-housed and the ill-fed, the ignorant and the fallen, the sick and the insane, the vagrant and the orphan, the dock-yard and the workshop, the factory and the mine. The modern historian calls it the 'New Philanthropy,' but he might have called it, with S. Paul, " the law of Christ."

Christian sentiment, we repeat, has gained an ever deepening hold on the foremost races of the world, whether professedly Christian or non-Christian. The voice which startled the wilderness is heard in the open street. The piety which once sought safety in the cloister finds it now in the crowd. The exhortations of the pulpit are the counsels of the Press. The persecutions of fiery zeal, the tests imposed by the strong, the disabilities endured by the weak, the corruptions of office, the violence of parties, the barbarities of warfare, the grosser severities of the law, the worst brutalities of sport, have now passed away. Religion has penetrated society ; total relapse is impossible. Man may still fall short of the measure of his stature, but no power for good or for evil will ever erase the code of Christian ethics out of the tablets of his heart. On this side we may say with Matthew Arnold that " Christianity is immortal ; it has eternal truth, inexhaustible value, a boundless future."

But "Christianity," says another writer, "is dying at the root." Christianity has many roots. Two, perhaps, are dying. Let us examine them.

First, the root of public worship. We have it on the testimony of an archdeacon (Farrar, *Sermon in Westminster Abbey*) that "not one tenth of the working classes frequent our churches, not three per cent. are partakers of our Holy Communion." The cause is not far to seek. Worship, to be real, must rest on an emotional basis, and, to be public, must rest on emotion which is public. There is the worship of a common joy, as when David cried, "Now bless the Lord your God. And all the congregation blessed the Lord, the God of their fathers, and bowed down their heads, and worshipped the Lord." There is the worship of a common distress, as when Ezra "blessed the Lord, the great God. And all the people answered, Amen, Amen, with lifting up their hands : and they bowed their heads, and worshipped the Lord with their faces to the ground. . . . . For all the people wept, when they heard the words of the law." As faiths have triumphed or suffered, worship has been glad and open in the upper air, or it has been secret and sad in catacomb and crypt. But there was that in all hearts which made them beat as the heart of one man. Emotion, grave or exultant, is the soul of worship ; worship without emotion is a harp with broken strings.

Now the working-man is not emotional, or only with the support of numbers and under special excitement.

At the same time he is too simple to understand a worship which is not fervid. He has not yet acquired the practised apathy, the lazy reverence, of the ordinary church-goer, or learned to accept divine service as an advisable, though tedious, formality; perhaps an occasional diversion. He is at home in a confraternity, in which all are of one social rank, but not in a congregation, in which distinctions of class cannot be concealed, and are often displayed. Let us confess it, worship is for most of us attendance at a place of worship, an act of compliance with duty, of external and mechanical obedience; at best a matter of private effort, not of common enthusiasm; and this is the secret of its decay.

Perhaps there are causes deeper still. It is thought by some that the Teutonic mind is averse from ceremony, that "as education advances the power of symbolism recedes," that "there is a growing suspicion of the value of all ritual," and that "bare truths simply stated have become more acceptable than any visible presentation." If all this be true of formal worship generally, especially is it true of an observance which more than any other demands sentiment and imagination—the observance of that Holy Communion of which not three per cent. of the working classes are partakers. It must often have seemed to the reader a remarkable fact that the Lord's Supper, though absolutely unconnected with any existing ceremony of the temple or of the synagogue at the time of its institution, should have become in the course of ages a purely ecclesiastical rite. It began in a dwelling-house, with the passing from hand to hand of the simplest elements of a simple meal.[1] The only vestment worn was a servant's apron ; the only sacrifice offered was one of stooping love—a most priestly act, but not a priestly function. The upper room is now a church, the table an altar, a familiar usage has become a mystery, social participation has passed into isolated reception, and the symbol of union into an instrument of divided grace. The change was slow and perhaps to each age imperceptible. The church-fabric grew out of the house as the congregation grew out of the household, and the former retained much of secular use as the latter retained much of family feeling. Even in this country, when the village-church was the place of meeting for every harmless purpose, the associations of the church were in some degree the associations of the home. The church is now reserved for the exercises of devotion and its most touching observance is devotional indeed, but the human warmth is gone. The bidding to the feast comes, not from mutual encouragement, but from official zeal ; approach to it is a test, and enjoyment a discipline. The guests are, constrained and reserved ; they meet without welcome and without apparent joy. In almost mournful order they advance and withdraw. For eighteen centuries and more the holy table, with its equal terms for all,

[1] Cf. Acts ii. 42. xx. 7. 1 Cor. xi. 20.

has been the symbol of fraternity, a constant and abiding testimony against the distinctions and inequalities of secular life. It ought therefore to be popular, but the people love it no more.

Et nos mutamur. The question, after all, is one, not only of religious imagination and of inherited tendency, but also of social fact and of present habit. As time goes on the modes of fellowship change. The associations connected with the 'breaking of bread' in token of goodwill were never as sacred or as strong in the West as in the East, but they were once stronger and more sacred amongst us than they are now. Therefore, even if the rite of Holy Communion could be brought back to something of the character of the common meal of the Christian family, it is doubtful whether an expansion of fellow-feeling would follow. We are not more selfish, but we are more self-contained, and the friendly pledges of our fathers are not the tokens of modern use. Certainly Nonconformists, with their greater liberty of action, have not been more successful in maintaining the Lord's Supper as a means of Christian contact. Shall we agree, then, reviewing what has here been said, that the spirit of sympathetic, congregational worship is all but dead?

The second dying root is the root of dogma. If we could compel every intelligent worshipper, as he left the church-porch, to stop and say how much of the Church's creed he actually believed, we should find that there was in the congregation as little unity of thought as there is union in feeling. There is an emotional formalism and there is also an " intellectual formalism." Just as we confess without sorrow, and pray without desire, and sing hymns of strained meaning, or of no meaning, without intention, so collectively we repeat articles of belief which singly we should hesitate to subscribe. We listen with a kind of numbed patience to propositions clothed in theological language which, stated nakedly, would fire us with indignation or freeze us with horror. We are content to take the greater part not too seriously and to let a creed so ancient stand a ruin rather than seem to touch it with profaning hand.

Authorised dogmatic teaching has but little hold on the popular mind. A poor man's creed is generally little more than a single clause. When he has done with the catechism, as a rule, he has done with the Prayer-book. He accepts baptism and confirmation for his children, but rarely on religious grounds ; and he is ready, on occasion, to affect dissent in its nearest local form, be its doctrine what it may. The more educated fly to scripture. They make and unmake doctrines with texts, as children play with letters.[1] Some profess to

---

[1] A curious instance of the extent to which contrary applications may be drawn from a single verse is found in Matt. v. 26. The text is used by Romanists to confirm the doctrine of purgatory, by Universalists to support the argument for final restitution, and by stricter Protestants to prove the certainty of eternal damnation. Similarly in Matt. v. 23, 24, some have found an argument for the perpetuity of Jewish sacrifice, whilst others

be guided by history, but history, like scripture, admits
of many selections.[1]   Some are guided by party, but
parties could not be unless men thought for themselves.
In fact we learn the dialects of the schools in which
we are taught and find out afterwards the difficulty of
speaking a dead language.   Or, to return to our first
metaphor, experience corrects opinion, and we feel at
last that the sap of religious life does not really flow
from the rival orthodoxies for which our fathers so
strangely fought and suffered and died.   Practically
they are as good as dead.

"What will it be in the end thereof?" is a question
often in our minds.   Of course the policy of a head
well buried in the sand has its advantages.   It is a
postponement of solution and that is the easiest of all
answers.   When the future of the Church rises with
ghost-like questioning, we lay it, pointing to the Church's
present activity.   This activity, after scrutiny, is found
to mean its activity as a philanthropic agency.   The
Church is the great almoner, the promoter of thrift, of
good manners, of mental improvement, of social amusement—that is enough.   "We are all church-men at
common law.   A man may never attend divine service, or
hold any theological position whatever, and yet honestly

declare that the verses point to the institution of the Roman
mass. 'Hic liber est in quo quærit sua dogmata quisque.'
[1] "Orthodox Christians may be divided into two broad
classes, one of which professes to base the Church upon the
Bible, the other the Bible upon the Church."—"*Supernat.
Religion.*"

uphold the church as a civilising and humanising agency. It is part of the ancient constitution of his country and does an immense amount of practical good which would not under other conditions, perhaps, be done at all. He is under no obligation to emphasise his membership, and we have no right to go behind his own definition of his own beliefs." This is the argument of ' *The Standard,*' a Journal beloved of good citizens and sound church-men. It is not a very direct answer to the pressing questions whether the National Church is, or is not, the accountable holder of a certain *fixed deposit ;* whether its value does, or does not, primarily and mainly depend on its sacraments, ceremonies, and doctrines; whether it has, or has not, the right to adapt its formularies to the "beliefs" of its members. It gives little comfort to those of the clergy whose consciences are wrung by many a vain endeavour to believe and teach honestly that which reason as honestly rejects. Let them, as ministers, by all means " serve tables," but their order is something more than a diaconate, and, as ministers, they have also a right to know definitely whether there is still " a ministry of the word," and whether it is any longer a matter of national concern. May they have a share in the liberty so generously granted to laymen ? May they also give their own definitions of their " beliefs" and ask that no one shall go behind them ? Must they drop to the rear of this movement of freer thought ? Shall they be living voices at last, or always phonographs of dead sound ? Ought they to keep within the four corners of the Prayer-book, or may they shut their eyes to another part of the ancient constitution of their country—the Ecclesiastical Courts? If the tabernacle is to be enlarged under the auspices of the Conservative Press, let us put in a petition that the cords may be lengthened all round. We do not wish ' *The Standard*' to retract its bold concessions, but we must smile at the curious attempt to swell the statistics against disestablishment by counting the heads of all those remarkable " churchmen" who are ready to accept the ministrations of the clergy anywhere but in church. A stronger point for disestablishment could hardly be made.

But Christianity, to return, is not only a plant of vigorous growth ; it is throwing out new roots in the place of those which are dying. In worship it makes. less of form, feeling more of the spirit ; in doctrine it contracts its beliefs, knowing better the limitations of knowledge ; in conduct it lowers an indefinitely high standard to the level of wider attainment. If its piety is less fervent, it is more enlightened ; if less concentrated, it is more practical. In short, religion is less conscious but more conscientious, less devout but more devoted, less introspective but more sensitive, less intense but more wholesome, showing less of personal energy and more of social effect. Its types of individual saintliness are not perhaps as clear, or as attractive, as in the past, but its character, as a whole, goes deeper every day into the morals of mankind. There are developments still to come, and change is as often a symptom of life as of decay. The tree will shed something of its outer form, but it will do this because it grows within.

CHAPTER VIII.

Conclusion.

If the reader will let his mind dwell calmly on the teaching of Christ here massed together, he will see religion as Christ saw it and as he meant it to be received. Let him say if it be not a religion sound and wholesome, manly and robust; suited to the necessities of a busy world as much as to the needs of an earnest soul; satisfying the reason; securing affection and obedience without straining them; practicable and sensible; safe from all serious attack and full of all good hope. Let him detach this religion from its after-developments; let him clear it from the endless subtleties of doctrine, from the endless refinements of duty, which have been poured into it; and he will find little that is abstruse or mystical, certainly nothing that is morbid or unnatural. Of many incidents in the Gospel narrative he may not be sure, many of the sayings attributed to Christ he may doubt, not a few of the statements made about him he may positively reject, but the gospel itself he cannot miss; it gleams like the merchant's goodly pearl, like the treasure uncovered in the field; it is historically and substantially true. The religion of Christ unfolds a noble plan—a plan of moral discipline, of social action, of spiritual endeavour. It covers the whole nature of man, develops his powers, hallows his relations, holds the secret of happiness and of wisdom, marks out firmly the path before his feet, and sketches something of that which lies beyond. A religion like this is not for the library, nor for the secret chamber, nor even for the sanctuary. A man may take it out as he walks, as Pilgrim took the roll from his bosom, and learn, as he did not, how to live in the world and not lose his way, and to think as hopefully of mankind as of himself.

One admission may frankly be made. The plan, as it stands, is set too high for human reach. Nothing has brought upon the Christian profession more scoffs than this. It aims, say its opponents, at an impossible standard, and the impossibility of attainment gives rise to a pretence of attainment which is hypocrisy. Now it is necessary to remember—First, that a moral teacher is obliged to present his system as an ideal; otherwise the treatment would be artistically imperfect and leave work for another hand. As in art the master carries the thoughts of his pupils beyond the actual achievements of art to the efforts of art never realised, so in ethics the teacher would have the learners view conduct, not only in its attainable, but also in its highest conceivable, excellence. Nor has any moral philosopher, whether heathen or Christian, even in an immoral age, ever submitted a code degraded to his own times. He does not select the best specimen that he can find amongst men as he knows them, but he projects man in the abstract to the utmost length of his capacities, and beyond them. Aristotle's completely virtuous character has never been seen in the flesh; Plato's model citizen was not a member of any known community; when Bacon says that "it is heaven on earth to have a man's mind move in charity, rest in providence, and turn upon the poles of truth," he hangs upon a sublime metaphor a being that was never born in earth or heaven. But we do not even smile. Similarly, when the members of the Kingdom appear as "Sons of the Most High," bidden to be "perfect" even as their Father in heaven is perfect, we know that they have never really walked in the likeness of men; though we have in them a vision of ourselves thrown out in larger form. By an instinct of perfection which will not be satisfied we are perpetually raising, for ourselves and for others, the standards of performance and of production in every department of life. And this is the practical effect of an idealised self, that, rightly understood, it stimulates action. Only by thinking of the best that can be done can we find the range of the best that we can do.

"He higher shoots who means the sky."

Nor can we allow that there is any justice in speaking of the Christian scheme as Utopian. The Kingdom is not Utopia. In Utopia the inhabitants are a finished product. They are turned out of hand by a too perfect education, by a too minute legislation, by a too paternal government. They are men with dislocated joints whose world is always a gymnasium. Therefore Utopia is the land of impracticable schemes for impossible beings. But the "children of light" have something of the nature of light. They move under discipline, but they move with the happy freedom of a force radiating from within. In them individualism and socialism have both a reasonable play.[1] Within their measure, separately and collectively, they shine more and more unto a perfect day.

The second point to be remembered is that many of the sayings of the Great Teacher are set in a frame of Eastern hyperbole. Exaggeration is always relative to the purpose with which it is used and to the sense ·in which it is received. In speech it is sometimes the language of compliment, sometimes of emphasis. It always supposes a mental deduction. When we are bidden to turn the unsmitten cheek to the smiter, we know at once what is meant and we are glad to have so simple an illustration of a difficult rule. The law of patience in one of its aspects—patience under insult— is revealed. But to take it literally, and to act upon it invariably, would be to throw other virtues out of action in ourselves and in others. Similarly with such figures

---

[1] "The individual view tends to selfishness and isolation when the larger scope of redemption is neglected; the social view tends to enthusiastic dreams, when the need of the transfiguration of every power of man is forgotten."—Westcott, *Epp. of S. John*, 252.

as that of the man who in his religious earnestness
hates his father living, and dead leaves him unburied.
The speaker and the hearers understood one another;
there was no need of explanation. Misconstruction was
prevented by a tacit adjustment. And no less is it
right, and much more is there need for us in this day
to make the necessary deduction, to find the right
equation, and to bring the purposely transcendent idea
within the not less intended lower line of possible
action.

Who can foresee the forms into which religion
purified and re-cast will run? After generations will
cling here and there to much that still lingers in the
reformed faith, just as our fathers clung to much now
discarded.[1] There are those who deliberately prefer
the miraculous element in religion, just as there are
minds which prefer the legendary element in history.
Evidence rarely touches them. Others, no doubt, have
by long and tender custom become so wedded to certain
forms of faith, that not without impossible violence
could they be unseated from their minds. But the
flow of change in religious thought, though it is thrown
back here and there by individual and denominational
resistance, with much noise and foam and seeming
strength, still passes on. Nor, from what we know of
the signs of to-day, is it quite impossible to forecast

[1] In many points true religion would not be comprehensible
by the ignorant, nor consolatory to them, nor guiding and sup-
porting for them."—Greg, *Creed of Christendom.*

something of the change of to-morrow. Men will believe that the love of God was incarnate in Jesus Christ, though they may not believe all that is now meant by the Incarnation ; they will cherish the hope of life upraised and renewed, though they claim no support for it from any historical Resurrection. They will remember that the homage which the Founder of their Faith demanded was the faithful acceptance of his call, and not the true appreciation of his Person. They will reverence him as the most God-like vision ever vouchsafed to mortal sight, but they will not think to follow him behind the clouds of their poor shortened gaze, and to say how or where or in what relation to the All-Father he exists. They will have also a more reverent view of the wise providence of God. They will better understand that He never springs surprises on the world. They will see that a design for the deliverance of man attested by a series of unattested, or insufficiently attested, miracles, and yet requiring belief in the miracles as a condition of deliverance, would be a design as unproved as it would be unworthy of proof. The proof of man's redemption is redemption. He feels himself to be free from much which once bound him. The manifestations of divine love are not without their marvels, but the antecedents are known ; they operate within view, and all men are witnesses. All things within and without us are full of revelation, but it is a revelation of increasing, not of diminishing, force, and it does not hang on the hazards of memory or of tradition, or on the origin or accuracy or fate of records, nor does it drop into the minds and drop from the pens of certain selected writers, nor is it preserved in the pages of one authorised book. Scripture, therefore, will be read under other light than its own. The Bible will need much sifting to be ever again popular, as the literature of any nation must be sifted to adapt it to later and public use. So too with Church-doctrine, whether founded on the strict letter of holy writ, or on the decrees of councils, or on the " passionate metaphors" of poets, or on the disquisitions of divines. Men will cease to torture themselves with perpetually revolving questions about sin, its origin and nature, the exact source of its remedies, the process of its expiation and the duration of its penalties. Salvation, they will know, is not a magical saving clutch from wrath to come, but the steady furtherance of a healthy condition (*salus*) of present life, the application of the laws of physical, mental, and spiritual well-being, the balanced play of every useful energy. Sin will be recognised as largely the result of immaturity, of constitutional tendency, of disabling circumstance, of tainting influence.[1] It will therefore be considered and treated as a morbid state of being. At the same time, because of the contributions which a man makes to his own condition, its guilt will not be denied, nor will its transgressions be condoned. Rather we may say that, under the influence of a finer conscience and a purer taste and a more active sympathy, society will resent sin more and

[1] The transmutation of disease into criminal instinct by heredity is now a question seriously considered in medical science.

more, not only as a social danger, but also as a disturbance of social happiness. Individual responsibility will not be lessened and public responsibility will be quickened. Forms of ill-doing and of ill-being which are stigmatised by general consent have a tendency to die out more than those which are prosecuted at law, or are denounced by the Church. It may, therefore, be expected that the more virulent types of sin will disappear. And, as its original nature is better understood, so will the character of its final penalty be better known. The reflex consequences of wrong-doing are never wholly arrested, just as its external effects are never wholly cancelled. Persistence in evil leads to conscious deterioration of character and depravation of taste, so that at last the capacity for enjoying goodness and its happiness is lost with the desire. This is sin's punishment. When this is rightly understood, there will be no necessity for religion to proclaim its penal laws. The certain prospect of self-inflicted loss, of separation from good hereafter by alienation from it now, of inability to live a higher life through the decay of higher energies—this prospect of a self-chosen gulf of self-destruction, of God-losing, not God-abandoned, death, would have more power to deter and to reform than the expectation of terrors which are always thought to be distant, indefinite, and perhaps not irrevocable. Nearly as awful as the pictures of souls in torment which frightened our childhood, and weigh upon us still, is the conception of a man who is his own devil and his own hell. The former we never perhaps quite believed, that the latter has been realised even in this. life who will deny? And yet for all who have done even their worst, whether living or dead, true religion, which is assured of nothing so much as of the depth of the divine mercy, will never refuse the wider hope. '

But a more powerful motive than the fear of loss and pain will be the yearning to do right in the presence of a righteous God. Prayer will be a habit of reference to the divine will, rather than of petition. Men will not think to move God to this or that, or by words to check or to accelerate, to divert or to undo, the sequence of events. Rather will they strive to change their own reluctant wills, seeking to learn the causes of good and ill and accepting all issues patiently which are beyond control. At the same time prayer will not cease to be the language of hope, of longing, of regret, of sub-mission, of resolve ; but it will breathe in the heart rather than speak itself from the lips. It will become less a matter of formal recitation at special hours, and in fixed postures, as men learn to regard and to use it more as a means of constant access than as the payment of a required offering at a stated time. In the same way the passive observance of the Day of Rest will pass into intelligent use. It will come as a welcome pause for happy communion with Nature and God and Man, after the example of him who on the sabbath-day " went through the corn fields," "entered into the synagogue," and "went into the house of one of the chief Pharisees." And for sacraments, the world will think perhaps again, with Luther, that those we have are too few, accepting every earnest token of mutual faith and love as of sacramental worth. Signs of dedication as the children of the Father, signs of union as brethren one with another—these there may be ; but assuredly the world will never return to the belief that particular material forms are the appointed channels of peculiar grace, or can in any way be "the connecting link between God and the human soul."

Pitiable to look upon is man in his religious history —pitiable in effort and in relapse—in faith, as in morals, half-angel and half-brute; worshipping now with silent awe and now with polluting rite, washing his hands in innocency and in blood, rearing altars or wrecking them, inventing the sacrifice of victims to save the sacrifice of sin, or new tortures for his flesh to save his soul from woe; presenting the Deity to himself in forms projected from his own lust, hiding under His honour the reproach of his own shame; in war and crusade full of zeal against idolatry, yet steeped in superstition, upholding the image of the Divine Son and doing the deeds of his murderers, honouring the Divine Mother and dishonouring living women; in a later age giving to torture and to death as heretics the martyrs of a future time, shuddering at science and pledged against reform; later still, dissecting his own faith into Articles and Confessions, proving by logic and by Scripture his damnation, and by neither his election—claiming from the beginning, and always, to know more than was ever revealed, the

counsels of the divine mind, the compacts of the
divine Persons, the modes of their relation and the
manners of their operation, the fulfilment of prophecy,
the day of final doom, the state of the departed, the
orders and ministries of angels and of devils, the inmost joys of heaven and all the pains of hell. Truly
man, as Goethe says, is more anthropomorphic than
he thinks.

But he is coming slowly to a better state. Church-
men are fond of saying that the Church is losing her
hold over the masses. It is for the masses to hold the
Church. The Church has been carried like a holy ark
by hands spiritual and by hands temporal in front of
the people ; her place is in the people.[1] Christianity,
let us say it again, is not an institution, but an
inspiration. The shrine is within. Outward expression there must be, by appointed hands and in
appointed ways, but this expression cannot be thrown
into a set ritual or fixed in a rigid creed. The religion
of Christ is the mind of Christ in man ; not within a
sacred enclosure, either in the individual or in the
state ; moving with supreme possession over every
part, employing every useful function, hallowing every
pure delight and furthering every noble end. It would
save, not souls, but men ; not out of the body, but in
the body ; not from the penalty of sin, but from the
power of sin ; not by and bye, but now ; not by
promising life in another world, but by giving it in

---

[1] In Numb. xii. 7 the people of God, by a happy phrase, is
termed the 'house' of God. Cf. Heb. iii. 6.

this. The Kingdom of God is Society in its best imaginable form. This form may never be fully attained, but, even with " a new heaven and a new earth," nothing can be righted hereafter which is neglected now.

> " We live by admiration, hope, and love;
> *And even as these are well and wisely fixed,*
> In dignity of being we ascend."

"Il y a cent ans, on ignorait ou l'on affectait d'ignorer qu'il y eût une histoire des dogmes."—*Reuss*.

"Maxima quæque ambigua sunt, dum alii quoquo modo audita pro compertis habent, alii vera in contrarium vertunt, et gliscit utrumque ;posteritate."—*Tacitus*.

"Luther emancipated us from tradition, but our escape from the still more intolerable burden of the letter is still to come."—*Lessing*.

"The New Testament exists to reveal Jesus Christ, not to establish the immunity of its writers from error." —*Matthew Arnold*.

APPENDIX I.

" We have reason to doubt whether prophetic inspiration ever results in the clear and definite knowledge of some single occurrence which is to take place in the future."—Professor Ladd, *Doctrine of Sacred Scripture,* i. p. 347.

" The prophet speaks always, in the first instance, to his own contemporaries : the message which he brings is intimately related with the circumstances of his time : his promises and predictions, however far they reach into the future, nevertheless rest upon the basis of the history of his own age."—Professor Driver, —*Introduction to the Literature of the Old Testament,* p. 224.

" The prophets make a direct claim to be the instruments of the Divine Spirit. No doubt their predictive knowledge is general, it is of the issue to which things tend."—*Lux Mundi,* p. 345, 2nd ed.

If the reader can accept these statements made by sound, if critical, Churchmen, statements which reduce the predictive element in prophetic writing to a minimum, he will have no difficulty in correcting the traditional ideas of ' prophecy ' and of ' fulfilment.'

In the common acceptance of the terms, 'prophecy' is designed reference to future definite acts, and 'fulfilment' is designed accomplishment of previous definite words. But a moderately careful study of the Old Testament will shew us that the predictions of the prophets are (1) references to contemporary events, or (2) efforts of sagacious calculation, or (3) natural, though sublime, anticipations of divine action; and even a slight examination of the passages quoted by the Evangelists will satisfy us that there is no neccessary connection between these passages and the alleged incidents to which they are applied. The relation is one of accidental correspondence, and the result, at best, is accidental illustration. Nor must we be misled by any theory of 'primary' and 'ultimate' applications, or any attempt to give to a simple utterance, when convenient, a two-fold significance and a double fulfilment.

Malachi iv. 5. " Behold, I will send you *Elijah the prophet* before the great and terrible day of the Lord [Jehovah] come."

Luke i. 17. [Gabriel to Zacharias] " He [John the Baptist] shall go before his face *in the spirit and power of Elijah* . . . . to make ready for the Lord a people prepared for him."

Matt. xi. 14. [Jesus to the multitudes] "If ye are willing to receive it, *this is Elijah which is to come.*"

Matt. xvii. 10. [Jesus to the disciples] "And he answered and said, *Elijah indeed cometh,*

and shall restore all things :
but I say unto you, that *Elijah
is come already,* and they knew
him not."

John i. 21. [Priests and
Levites to John] "And they
asked him, What then ? Art
thou Elijah ? *And he saith,
I am not.*"

Malachi meant, the Scribes taught, and the people
believed, that Elijah would appear in person and precede the coming of Jehovah Himself to judgment. By
a series of accommodations the actual Elijah becomes
(before his birth) Elijah-like John, but still the fore-
runner of God ; the prophecy is then (during his
lifetime) applied to John exclusively ; after his death
it is divided between him and the real Elijah still to
come ; and as a crowning confusion, John himself
shows, in his answer to the priests, that he is ignorant
that he is Elijah in any sense.

Malachi iii. 2. "Behold, *I*
[Jehovah] send my messen-
ger, and he shall prepare the
way before me."

Luke i. 76. [Zacharias to
John] "Yea, and thou, child,
shalt be called the prophet of
the Most High : For thou
shalt go before the face of
the Lord to make ready *his*
ways."

Luke vii. 27. [Christ to
the multitudes] "This is he
of whom it is written, Behold,
I send my messenger before
thy face, Who shall prepare
thy way before *thee.*" Cf.
Matt. xi. 10. Mark i. 2.

In these passages the prophecy is first applied to
John the Baptist, as the messenger of the Most High,
and then, by giving a different turn to the pronouns,
the application is extended and Jehovah's messenger
announces the coming, not of Jehovah, but of Christ.[1]

Isaiah xl. 3. "The voice of
one that crieth, Prepare ye in
the wilderness the way of the
Lord, make straight in the
desert a high way *for our
God.*"

Matt. iii. 3, Mark i. 3,
Luke iii. 4, John i. 23.

In these passages the prophecy is applied by the Evangelist to the Baptist, or by
the Baptist to himself, but in
each case as the messenger of
Jehovah.

Micah v. 2. "But thou,
Bethlehem, ... out of thee
shall one come forth unto me
that is to be ruler in Israel,
.... [*and he shall deliver
us from the Assyrian*"].

Matt. ii. 4. "He inquired
of them where the Christ
should be born. And they
said unto him, In Bethlehem
of Judæa : for thus it is
written by the prophet."

The concluding words, in
brackets, are an inseparable
part of the prophecy and must
not be omitted in the claim
to fulfilment. For evidence
against Bethlehem as the
birth-place of Christ, see
Matt. xiii. 57, Mark vi. 4,
Luke iv. 23, 24, John i. 45,
46 : vii. 41, 42.

[1] "Patris sermo ad Filium," is Bengel's note on Matt. xi. 10 (!).

Isaiah vii. 14. " Behold, a virgin shall conceive, and bear a son, and shall call his name Immanuel."

Matt. i. 22, 23. "Now all this is come to pass, that it might be fulfilled which was spoken by the Lord through the prophet, saying, Behold, the virgin shall be with child, and shall bring forth a son."

The prophet's words were never applied to Messiah by the Jews for the sufficient reason that they involved the promise of fulfilment within two years. A prophecy cancelled by fulfilment can hardly be revived as the prediction of another event.

The word *Almah*, rendered 'virgin,' means a young woman ripe for marriage.

Hosea xi. 1. "When *Israel* was a child, then I loved him and called my son out of Egypt."

Matt. ii. 15. "That it might be fulfilled which was spoken by the Lord through the prophet, saying, Out of Egypt did I call my son."

The words of Hosea are a simple reference to the bringing of Israel out of Egypt by Moses."

Jeremiah xxxi. 15. "A voice is heard in Ramah, lamentation and bitter weeping, Rachel weeping for her children, because they are not."

Matt. ii. 17, 18. "Then was fulfilled that which was spoken by Jeremiah the prophet, saying," &c.

Here, again, there can be no positive connection between the slaughter of Benjamites, or Ephraimites, at the Ramah in Benjamin or in Mount Ephraim, described by the prophet, and the massacre of Innocents at Bethlehem.

Zechariah xi. 12, 13. "And I said unto them, If ye think good, *give me my hire;* and if not, forbear. So they weighed for my hire thirty pieces of silver. And the Lord said unto me, Cast it unto the potter, the goodly price that I was prised at of them. And I took the thirty pieces of silver, and cast them unto the potter, in the house of the Lord."

Matt. xxvii. 9, 10. "Then was fulfilled that which was spoken by Jeremiah the prophet, saying, And they took the thirty pieces of silver, the price of him that was priced, whom certain of the children of Israel did price; and they gave them for the potter's field, as the Lord appointed me."

In the original passage it is the prophet who is prised, and it is his hire, not his life, that is valued.

Psalm xxii. 18. "They part my garments among them, And upon my vesture do they cast lots."

John xix. 23, 24. "The soldiers therefore, when they had crucified Jesus, took his garments, and made four parts, to every soldier a part; and also the coat: now the coat was without seam, woven from the top throughout. They said therefore one to another, " Let us not rend it, but cast lots for it, whose it shall be : that the scripture might be fulfilled, which saith,

They parted my garments among them,

And upon my vesture did they cast lots."

But, by the well-known synonymous parallelism of Hebrew Poetry, the two lines express the same idea and, probably, no distinction is intended between ' garments ' and ' vesture.'

If this be so, a miscon-construction of the original passage would seem to have led to the minute distinctions given above, if not to the fashioning of the whole narrative. Cf. verses 1, 7, 8, 16, of the Psalm and Matt. xxvii. 35, where reference to prophecy is omitted in the oldest MSS.

Psalm xxxiv. 19, 20. " Many are the afflictions of the righteous : But the Lord delivereth him out of them all. He keepeth all his bones : Not one of them is broken."

John xix. 36. " For these things came to pass, that the scripture might be fulfilled, A bone of him shall not be broken."

The Psalmist speaks of the

preservation of the *living*, not of the dead, from violence. The case to which the Evangelist applies the words would. prove rather the non-fulfilment than the fulfilment of "the scripture." If the reference be to Exodus xii. 46, the illustration would be equally unmeaning.

Zechariah xii. 10. "And I will pour upon the house of David, and upon the inhabitants of Jerusalem, the spirit of grace and of supplication ; and they shall look unto me [Jehovah] whom they have pierced."

John xix. 37. "And again another scripture saith, They shall look on him whom they pierced."

The prophet says, figuratively, that Jehovah has been pierced by the transgressions of His people. The Evangelist applies the words, literally, to Jesus pierced by the soldier's spear.

Judges xiii. 5. "The child [Samson] shall be a *Nazirite* unto God," *i.e.* bound by a Nazirite's vow.

Matt. ii. 22, 23. "He [Joseph] withdrew into the parts of Galilee, and came and dwelt in a city called *Nazareth :* that it might be fulfilled which was spoken by the prophets, that he should be called a *Nazarene.*"

It is of course possible that

the words may be taken from some lost, or traditional, 'prophecy,' but it is difficult not to believe that the writer had in his mind the passage from the Book of Judges given above. Had the Evangelist intended to mark any connection between *Nazareth*, 'the city of *branches*,' and the term '*Branch*,' as applied to the Messiah, he would, as Olshausen admits, have quoted a distinct passage from the prophets, where the term occurs—*e.g.*, Isaiah xi. 1. But even allowing, with Delitzsch and others, that there is a reference to such places as Isaiah xi. 1 ; liii. 2, it is not easy to see how local association with 'the city of branches' could in any edifying sense be a 'fulfilment' of the statement that Messiah himself would be a 'Branch' or 'Root.'

APPENDIX II.

Orthodox commentators, when they speak of the discrepancies of the Gospels, seem generally to have in their minds certain very small and unimportant variations. A great deal of argument is spent in meeting the questions whether one blind man was healed at Jericho, or two blind men, and on entering the town, or on leaving it; whether there were two Gadarene demoniacs, or one alone ; whether the First Evangelist is right who speaks of an ass and its colt, or the other Three who mention the foal only. It is thought to be enough if they reduce the opposition between the various accounts of the bearing of the Cross, of the denials of Peter, of the inscription on the Cross, of the hour of the Crucifixion, of the angel, or angels, at the Sepulchre, of the stone rolled away. But there is really no necessity for this anxious defence of small points from which the attack has long since retired. Differences like these are of little account on either side of the argument. Inconsistencies in matters of detail may always be expected and allowed for in any two reports of any one event, not committed to writing at the time of the event. Nor is strict chronological order to be looked for from reporters who have not had a single note to guide them in the sequence of events. But when the opposed statements, taken together, are not variations, but contradictions, that is to say, are contradictory on historical, logical, or moral grounds, then the discrepancy is of another and more serious nature. The diversity then lies, not in the fringe of circumstance, but in the central subject-matter. The difference becomes a question, not of more or less accuracy in description, but of the reporter's right to be heard in evidence at all. Few readers of Scripture will be at the trouble of reading the Gospels, so to speak, collaterally. They read them consecutively, with an occasional reference to confirmatory passages. But honest study demands attention to the whole text, to places which are divergent quite as much as to those which are parallel. The following table of opposed verses is very far from being complete, but it illustrates the writer's meaning and may be helpful to others who are labouring in the same field. As an example of the value of this comparative study let the reader refer to the passages on the *Parousia* contrasted on p. 170. The juxtaposition throws out the distinct conceptions which were in the minds of successive transcribers as to the scene and time of Christ's Coming.

Criticism is concentrating itself more and more on the pure subject-matter of the Four Gospels. It is no longer enough to adduce external and internal evidence for the mere authenticity of each document.

Of portions of those documents in their present form we may say that, though "an angel from heaven" preached them, they ought not to be believed. In the columns here contrasted it will be seen that there are many passages which are simply cancelled out by their unsoundness on logical or moral grounds. By this process of reduction; by testing the inherent worth as well as the historical credibility of the various statements; by applying tests far more searching than the amount of verbal correspondence in Justin Martyr, or the number of hints and clues of authorship furnished by the compositions themselves, we shall simplify the problem and come, perhaps, at last to those certain results which may be accepted without question and preserved without shame.[1]

Matt. i. 1—17.   Luke iii. 23—38.

In these two genealogies, from David downwards, there are only two names in which they agree; in the former several generations are omitted in order to secure the symmetrical arithmetical result mentioned in *v.* 17; it is said that the "childless" Jechoniah (Jer. xxii. 30) "begat" Shealtiel, whilst, in the second, Shealtiel is the son of Neri and derives his descent

[1] "J'ai examiné avec une attention scrupuleuse les oppositions contradictoires que certains critiques ont prétendu voir dans la narration multiple des quatres Évangelistes; jamais je n'ai pu les découvrir"(!)—Père Didon, *Jésus Christ.*

from David through Nathan; and, lastly, they do not even meet in Joseph's father, whose true name and line of succession are left undetermined. See, further, Appendix III.

Matt. i. 18. " Before they came together she was found with child of the Holy Ghost."

Matt. xiii. 55. " Is not this the carpenter's son ?"

Mark vi. 3. " Is not this the carpenter, the son of Mary, and brother of James ?"

Luke ii. 27. " The parents brought in the child Jesus."

Luke ii. 48. " Thy father and I have sought thee sorrrowing."

Luke iv. 22. " And they said, Is not this Joseph's son ?"

John i. 45. " Jesus of Nazareth, the son of Joseph."

John vi. 42. " Is not this Jesus, the son of Joseph, whose father and mother we know ?"

Matt. ii. 1. " When Jesus was born in *Bethlehem* of Judæa."

John vii. 28. " Jesus therefore cried in the temple, teaching and saying, ye both know me, and know whence I am."

They could only connect him with Nazareth, and when in vv. 41, 42, his birth in

Galilee is asserted to be inconsistent with Messiahship, the
statement is allowed by Jesus
to pass uncorrected ; though
there could be no better
opportunity for declaring the
birth in Bethlehem and the
fulfilment of prophecy. Cf.
Luke iv. 23.

Matt. ii. 4, 5. " Herod inquired of them where the
Christ should be born. And
they said unto him, In Bethlehem of Judæa."

John vii, 27. " When
the Christ cometh, no one
knoweth whence he is."

Matt. ii. 14. " And he
arose and took the young
child and his mother by
night, and departed into
Egypt, and was there until
the death of Herod."

Luke ii. 39. " And when
they had accomplished all
things that were according
to the law of the Lord, they
returned into *Galilee*, to their
own city Nazareth."

Matt. ii. 22. " Being warned
of God in a dream, he *withdrew* into the parts of Galilee,
and *came and dwelt* in a city
called Nazareth."

This Evangelist seems to
be of opinion that Joseph
hitherto had lived in Bethlehem.

Luke ii. 39. " And when
they had accomplished all
things that were according
to the law of the Lord, they
returned into Galilee, *to their
own city* Nazareth."

This writer supposes that
Joseph habitually lived in
Nazareth.

Matt. iii. 11. " I indeed baptise you *with water unto repentance :* but he that cometh after me . . . . *he shall baptise you with the Holy Ghost and with fire.*"

In Acts xi. 16, these words are given as " the word of the Lord," not of the Baptist. See i. 5.

John iv. 1.

The writer of the Fourth Gospel here speaks of a baptism by *water* under the direction of Jesus, when " the Holy Ghost was not yet given" (vii. 39). The First Evangelist could hardly, then, have known this second baptism " with water unto repentance."

Matt. iii. 17. " And lo, a voice out of the heavens, saying, This is my beloved Son."

John v. 37. " Ye have neither heard his voice at any time, nor seen his form."

Matt. vii. 22, 23. " Many will say to me in that day, Lord, Lord, did we not prophesy by thy name, and by thy name cast out devils, and by thy name do many mighty works ?   And then will I profess unto them, I never knew you : depart from me, ye that work iniquity."

" 28. " When Jesus ended these words, *the multitudes were astonished* at his teaching."

Mark i. 34. iii. 12. viii. 30.

The First Evangelist relates what is practically *a public assumption at a very early date* of Messianic dignity and power, and this open assertion of claim is quite inconsistent with the injunctions of secrecy with regard to that claim related by the Second Evangelist in the passages cited above.

Matt. x. 23. " When they persecute you in this city, flee unto the next : for verily I say unto you, *Ye shall not have gone through the cities of Israel*, till the Son of man be come."

Matt. xvi. 28. " There be *some of them that stand here*, which shall in no wise taste of death, till they see the Son of man coming in his kingdom."

Matt. xxiv. 34. " Verily I say unto you, *This generation* shall not pass away, till all these things be accomplished."

It is impossible to separate this last verse from the words which precede and follow it (vv. 30, 31, 36) and to apply it, in a special and narrower sense, to the destruction of Jerusalem. The difficulty is felt by those commentators who interpret the passage as meaning that the *Jewish race* would not pass away till the end. This would be a safe, but not very prophetic declaration.

Matt. xxiv. 14. " And this gospel of the kingdom shall be preached *in the whole world* for a testimony unto *all the nations; and then shall the end come*."

Mark xiii. 10. " And the gospel must first be preached unto *all the nations*."

Matt. xxiv. 36. " But of that day and hour *knoweth no one*, not even the angels of heaven, neither the Son, but the Father only."

These passages appear to have been thrown in by later transcribers to amend the too precisely worded statements of earlier tradition and to explain their non-fulfilment.

Matt. xi. 12. "From the days of John the Baptist *until now* the kingdom of heaven suffereth violence, and men of violence take it by force."

Supposed to be spoken when the Baptist is still living ; but the passage is evidently an editorial comment of later date.

Matt. xii. 38. "Then certain of the scribes and Pharisees answered him, saying, Master, we would see a sign from thee." Cf. xvi. 1. Mark viii. 11. Luke xi. 16. John ii. 18. 1 Cor. i. 22.

Matt. xii. 39. "But he answered and said unto them, An evil and adulterous *generation* seeketh after a sign ; and there shall no sign be given to *it* but the sign of Jonah the prophet." Cf. xvi. 4. Mark viii. 12. Luke xii. 57.

The evidence of these passages would point, if anywhere, to an early tradition that Christ did not give 'signs' of striking miraculous power. This is borne out by the " works and wonders and signs" of Acts ii. 22, explained by x. 38. In both cases S. Peter is the eye-witness and the speaker.

Matt. xii. 40. "As Jonah was three days and three nights in the belly of the whale ; so shall the Son of

(Jonah i. 17.) Does any one now seriously suppose that this passage describes a

man be three days and three nights in the heart of the earth."

real, historical event ? But, if " there are indications that the narrative is not strictly historical," (Driver, *Introd. to Lit. of O.T.*), if it bears marks of fiction as patently as any of the tales in the Thousand and One Nights, (Cheyne, *Theological Review*, 1877), then the unreal story could in no justifiable way be adduced as a type of the Resurrection. There must be a correspondence of reality in the two miraculous events, if one is to be a ' sign' of the other.

Matt. xii. 40. " As Jonah was three days and three nights in the belly of the whale, so shall the Son of man be *three days and three nights* in the heart of the earth."

No reckoning can give more than one day and two nights. Moreover, the Third Gospel (Luke xi. 30) gives a very different turn to "the sign of Jonah."

Matt. xiii. 11 (cf. Mark iv. 10—13. Luke viii. 9, 10). " Unto you it is given to know the *mysteries* of the kingdom of heaven." Cf. 51.

Is this borne out by the

Matt. x. 27. "What I tell you in the darkness, speak ye in the light : and what ye hear in the ear, proclaim upon the housetops."

Luke xii. 2. " There is

many blunders and misconceptions on the part of the Apostles which are afterwards recounted in the Gospel narrative ? The words belong to a later day when the teaching of the Master and the facts of his life had been fitted into the frame-work of the Old Testament by those who were " mighty in the scriptures," and interwoven with the dark sayings of the prophets. Only by proof drawn from ancient scripture, and by the unwrapping of its 'mysteries,' could the new Faith be presented successfully to Jews. See Acts ix. 22 ; xvii. 3 ; xviii. 28. Thus the simple " *disciple* to the kingdom of heaven" came to be a learned "*scribe*" (Matt. xiii. 52), and the open message of the gospel a system of cryptograms.

nothing covered up, that shall not be revealed : and hid, that shall not be known." Cf. viii. 17.

Matt. xiii. 41. " The Son of man shall send forth his angels." . . 51. " Have ye understood all these things ? They say unto him, Yea."

The mention by Jesus of "his angels " so early in his ministry, and so long before the crisis marked by Peter's confession in ch. xvi. is scarcely possible. If they "understood all these things," what need was there for the 'Whom say ye that I am?' as a critical question later on? Verses 40, 41, 49, 50 have all the appearance of editorial comment.

Matt. xiv. 15—21. The Feeding of the Five Thousand:—*v.* 17. "And they say unto him, We have here but five loaves, and two fishes."

Matt. xv. 33. "And the disciples say unto him, Whence should we have so many loaves in a desert place, as to fill so great a multitude?"

The question could hardly present itself after the former miracle already witnessed.

Matt. xvi. 13. "Who do men say that the Son of man is?"

Matt. ix. 27 ; xii. 23 ; xv. 22.

According to these passages the common talk was sufficiently known already.

Matt. xvi. 15. "Who say ye that I am?"

Matt. xiv. 33. "And they that were in the boat worshipped him, saying, Of a truth thou art the Son of God."

According to this passage the disciples had already made their confession.

Matt. xvi. 16. "And Simon Peter answered and said, Thou art the Christ, the Son of the living God."

Mark viii. 29. "Thou art the Christ." Luke ix. 20, "The Christ of God." John vi. 69, "The Holy One of God."

Matt. xvi. 16, 17. "And Jesus answered and said unto him, Blessed art thou, Simon Bar-Jonah ; for *flesh and blood hath not revealed it unto thee*, but my Father which is in heaven."

John i. 41. "He (*Andrew*) findeth first his own brother *Simon*, and saith unto him, We have found the Messiah."

And, according to this Evangelist, Jesus had, before Peter's confession, been already owned and confessed as Messiah by Nathanael, John the Baptist (see especially i. 34.), and many Samaritans.

Matt. xvi. 20 (Cf. xvii. 9, Mark viii. 30, Luke ix. 21, 22).

Secrecy as to Messiahship enjoined.

John iii. 13, iv. 26, v. 18, vi. 27, x. 25.

Messiahship openly asserted.

Matt. xvi. 28. "There be some of them that stand here, *which shall in no wise taste of death*, till they see the Son of man coming in his kingdom."

Either the words were never uttered, or they were never fulfilled. Only by an effort of despair can the fulfilment be found in the Destruction of Jerusalem, or in the Transfiguration.

Matt. xvi. 18. "And I also say unto thee, that thou art *Peter*, and upon this *rock* I will build my church. *I will give unto thee* the keys of the kingdom of heaven."

Cf. Mark viii. 29, Luke ix. 20, in which places this verse is not given.

Matt. xviii. 18. "Verily I say unto you, What things soever *ye shall bind* on earth shall be bound in heaven : and what things soever *ye shall loose* on earth shall be loosed in heaven." (Cf. John xx. 23).

This passage practically neutralises the verse which confers special powers on Peter. Moreover, the fanciful emphasis laid upon a name which had been given long before (Mark iii. 16, John i. 42) ; the use of the word "church ;" the absence of all reference in S. Paul's Epistles and in the Apocalypse to any such preeminence, and in the writings of the next century to any such foundation—all seem to mark the passage as an insertion by an Ebionite partisan in honour of the Apostle of the Circumcision.[1]

---

[1] This view is only confirmed by the following striking, but solitary, statement in the Clementine Homilies (17, 19, quoted in Anger's *Synopsis*): πρὸς γὰρ στερεὰν πέτραν ὄντα με, θεμέλιον ἐκκλησίας, ἐναντίος ἀνθέστηκάς μοι. Cf. *Ep. ad Jac.* § 1, τῆς ἐκκλησίας θεμέλιος ἔιναι ὁρισθείς.

Matt. xvii. 3. "And behold, there appeared unto them Moses and Elijah talking with him."

Matt xvii. 10. "And his disciples asked him, saying, Why then say the scribes that Elijah must first come?"

But, if they had just seen him on the mount of the Transfiguration, Elijah had come. Moreover, in *v.* 12, the literal coming of Elijah is rejected and he is said to have come already in the person of John the Baptist.

Matt. xvii. 9. "And as they were coming down from the mountain, Jesus commanded them, saying, Tell the vision to no man, until the Son of man be risen from the dead." Cf. xvi. 21, xx. 19. Mark viii. 31, ix. 31, x. 34. Luke ix. 22, xviii. 33, xxiv. 6, 7.

Mark xvi. 14, "And afterwards he was manifested unto the eleven themselves as they sat at meat; and he upbraided them with their unbelief and hardness of heart, because they believed not them which had seen him after he was risen."

Luke xxiv. 8. "And they" (the women) "remembered his words."

Luke xxiv. 11. "And these words appeared in their" (the apostles') "sight as idle talk; and they disbelieved them."

Thus the women, to whom no direct information had been given, remembered everything, whilst the apostles, who had specially and repeatedly received it, remembered nothing. Cf. Matt. xxviii. 17.

Matt. xvii. 22, 23. " And while they abode in Galilee, Jesus said unto them, The Son of man shall be delivered up into the hands of men ; and they shall kill him, *and the third day he shall be raised up*." Cf. xx. 17. Mark x. 33.   Luke xviii. 31.

John xx. 9. " For *as yet they knew not* the scripture, that he must rise again from the dead."

" The scripture " is said to be Ps. xvi. 10. " For thou wilt not leave my soul to Sheol ; neither wilt thou suffer thine holy *(*or, *godly*, or, *beloved)* one[1] to see corruption *(*or, *the pit)*."

Matt. xviii. 2. " He called to him a little child, and set him in the midst of them."

Matt. xviii. 5. (Cf. Mark ix. 33—50). " Whoso shall receive one such little child in my name receiveth me : but whoso shall cause one of these little ones *which believe on me* to stumble," &c.

The meaning hovers between the imitation of children and the treatment of weak and humble converts in the Christian congregation. This mingling of two ideas

[1] Why ' holy one' in the Psalm and ' Holy One' when the words are cited in Peter's sermon, Acts ii. 27 ?

seems to point to an expansion at a later date of some original saying based on a real incident.

A similar instance of subsequent extension in view of subsequent events seems to be furnished by the Parable of the Wicked Husbandmen, Matt. xxi. 33—46. Mark xii. 1—12. Luke xx. 9—16, and there are even marks of hesitation in the arrangement of the speakers in Matt. xxi. 41, compared with Luke xx. 16.

The most striking example of this adaptation of early injunctions to later needs is found in the relation of the Sending forth of the Seventy, Luke x. 1—16, compared with the Sending of the Twelve, Matt. x. 5—23.

Matt. xviii. 17. "And if he refuse to hear them, tell it unto the *church;* and if he refuse to hear the church also, let him be unto thee as the Gentile and the publican." Cf. Matt. xvi. 18.

The word " church " must have crept in from a later age. The idea of local "churches," with fixed powers and formal organization, is,

N 2

at this period, entirely foreign to the conception of the Kingdom. Compare the use of the word "prophet" in Matt. vii. 15. x. 41. (cf. 2. Peter ii. 1).

Matt. xix. 12. "There are eunuchs, which made themselves eunuchs for the kingdom of heaven's sake."

Taken literally, or figuratively, of the celibate life, the passage bears the stamp of a later age.

Matt. xxi. 12, 13 (cf. Mark xi. 15—18, Luke xix. 45, 46).

Cleansing of the temple placed at the close of Christ's ministry.

John ii. 13—17.

Cleansing of the temple placed at the beginning of Christ's ministry.[2]

Matt. xxi. 19, 20.

The withering of the barren fig-tree takes place immediately, and is at once commented upon by the disciples.

Mark xi. 20, 21.

The fact is not observed, nor is surprise expressed, until twenty-four hours later.

Matt. xxii. 43. "How then doth *David* in the Spirit call him Lord?" Cf. Mark xii. 36, 37. "*David himself* said in

In Psalm cx. 1, it is, "The LORD saith unto my *lord*," and of the 'lord,' or king, it

[1] Tatian in his Diatessaron gives only one Cleansing, and that towards the end of the ministry.

the Holy Spirit, ...
. . *David himself* called him
Lord." Cf. Luke xx. 42,
44.

The whole argument turns
upon the assumption that
David and no other wrote
the particular Psalm from
which the words quoted in
these passages are taken.[1]

it is said, at the close of the
Psalm, "He shall fill the
places with dead bodies ; He
shall strike through the head
in many countries. He shall
drink of the brook in the
way (in pursuit of his enemies), Therefore shall he lift
up his head." An earthly
monarch of this coarse type
might easily be David's lord
and son. But it is really a
prophet who speaks, and he
speaks of the ideal theocratic
king.

Matt. xxiii. 12. " Whoso-
ever shall exalt himself shall
be humbled ; and whosoever
shall humble himself shall be
exalted."

Luke xiv. 11. xviii. 14.

The words in the First
Gospel are stated to have
been spoken in the temple,
with a general application ;
by the Third Evangelist they
are specially connected with
two distinct and earlier occasions.

. [2] " This Psalm can hardly have been composed by David ;"
Driver, *Introduction to the Literature of the Old Testament*. 1891,
p. 362. Professor Cheyne places the composition of the Psalm
about 142 B.C. ; *Bampton Lectures*, 1889.

Matt. xxiii. 35.
Barachiah for Jehoiada.

Matt. xxvii. 9.
Jeremiah for Zechariah.

Mark ii. 26.
Abiathar for Ahimelech.

Admitted errors. In two
of the three passages the
words are said to have been
spoken by Jesus. Is the original transcriber at fault, or
the later copyist, or neither?

Matt. xxiv. 15. " When
therefore ye see the abomi-
nation of desolation, which
was spoken of by *Daniel the
prophet.*"

(Daniel ix. 27 ; xii. 11.)

" In face of the facts presented by the Book of Daniel,
the opinion that it is the work
of Daniel himself cannot be
sustained." (Driver, *Intr. to
Lit of O. T.* p. 467.)

" Jesus, the son of Sirach
(writing c. 200 B.C.), in his
enumeration of Israelitish
worthies, c. 44—50, though
he mentions Isaiah, Jere-
miah, Ezekiel, and (collectively) the Twelve Minor
Prophets, is silent as to
Daniel." (*Do. do.*)

Matt. xxvi. 25. " And
Judas, which betrayed him,
answered and said, Is it I,
Rabbi ? He saith unto him,
Thou hast said."

Matt. xxvi. 22. " And they
began to say unto him every
one, Is it I, Lord ? And he
answered and said, *He that
dipped his hand with me* in

the dish, the same shall betray me."

After the question and answer of this twenty-second verse, and the completed act of dipping, the inquiry of Judas in the twenty-fifth verse would be superfluous. In any case by this time the truth must have been known to all.

There is a further dis-crepancy with John xiii. 26, "He it is *for whom I shall dip the sop*, and give it him." Here the circumstances are adjusted to the passage from the 41st Psalm cited in ver. 18, and declared to have been thus "fulfilled," "He that eateth *my* bread."

Other MSS. of the Fourth Gospel revert to the older form of the tradition and read : " He that eateth *his* bread *with me;*" cf. Mark xiv. 18. There are many such instances of incident shaped by supposed prophecy.

Matt. xxvii. 5. "And he (Judas) cast down the pieces of silver into the sanctuary, and departed."

[Acts i. 18. "Now this man obtained a field with the reward of his iniquity."]

Matt. xxvii. 35. "That it might be fulfilled which was spoken by the prophet, They parted my garments among them, and upon my vesture did they cast lots."

Not found in ℵ. A. B. D. and therefore omitted in the Revised Version.

Matt. xxvii. 63. [The chief priests and the Pharisees to Pilate]. "Sir, we remember that that deceiver said, while he was yet alive, After three days I rise again."

The enemies of Jesus, to whom no direct intimation had ever been given, "remember."

Luke xxiv. 11. "And these words" (announcing the fact of the resurrection) "appeared in their sight as idle talk ; and they disbelieved them."

His friends who had been specially instructed and frequently reminded (Matt. xvi. 21 ; xvii. 23 ; xx. 19) "disbelieve."

Matt. xxviii. 9, 10. "And behold, *Jesus met them*, saying, All hail. . . . go tell my brethren."

Mark xvi. 9, 10. "*He appeared* first to Mary Magdalene. . . . She went and told them that had been with him."

· John xx. 14, 18. "She (Mary Magdalene) turned herself back, *and beholdeth*

Luke xxiv. 22, 33, 34. "Moreover certain women of our company amazed us, having been early at the tomb ; and when they found not his body, they came, saying, that they had also seen *a vision of angels*, which said that he was alive. . . . And they rose up that very hour and returned to Jerusalem, and found the eleven gathered together, *and them*

Jesus standing.' . . . .
Mary Magdalene cometh and
telleth the disciples, I have
seen the Lord."

that were with them, saying,
The Lord is risen indeed, and
hath appeared to Simon."[1]

The Third Evangelist knows nothing of any appearance of the risen Christ to women, and excludes all testimony from them to that effect. In this he is in agreement with S. Paul who (i. Cor. xv. 5.) also omits all mention of women and makes the appearance to Peter the first in the order. On the interesting question whether the apostle, in classing himself with those to whom Christ had appeared, meant that the manifestations were in every case, as in his own, facts of spiritual revelation and not of bodily presentation, the reader may consult Weizsäcker, *Das Apostolische Zeitalter*, 5—11.

Matt. xxviii. 10, 16, 17.
" Then saith Jesus unto
them, Fear not : go tell my
brethren that they depart

Luke xxiv. 36 ⎱ Appearance
John xx. 19 ⎰ to ten apostles
Mark xvi. 14 ⎱ Appearance
John xx. 26 ⎰ to the eleven.

[1] The other Evangelists make no mention of this separate appearance to Peter.

into Galilee, *and there shall they see me.*"

" But the eleven disciples went into Galilee, unto the mountain where Jesus had appointed them. And when they saw him, they worshipped him : but some doubted."

This writer knows nothing of the appearance to the ten, nor of that to the eleven (seven days after) in Jerusalem, but believes, apparently, that the eleven apostles went immediately to Galilee and there on a mountain received the first and only revelation of their risen Lord. There is nothing to confirm the Galilæan tradition beyond the abrupt and confused supplement in the appendix to the Fourth Gospel, xxi. 1—24.

Matt. xxviii. 19, 20. " Go ye, therefore, and make disciples of *all the nations*, baptizing them into the name of the Father and of the Son and of the Holy Ghost."

Matt. x. 23. " Verily I say unto you, Ye shall not have gone through *the cities of Israel* till the Son of man be come." Cf. *v.* 5.

The closing words are clearly of later date than the main body of the First

Gospel and belong to a later period of thought, when a wider conception of the extent and range of the Kingdom (based, perhaps, on the Parables of the Kingdom) had arisen.

Further evidence is supplied by the abrupt .introduction of the full baptismal formula not yet in use and not found in connection with baptism in any other part of the New Testament. See Acts ii. 38 ; viii. 16, 37 ; xix. 5 ; Rom. vi. 3 ; 1 Cor. i. 13 ; Gal. iii. 27.[1] Cf. 2 Cor. xiii. 13.

Mark i. 13. " And he was in the wilderness *forty days tempted* of Satan." Cf. Luke iv. 1, 2.

Matt. iv. 2, 3. " And when he had fasted forty days and forty nights, he *afterward* hungered. *And the tempter came* and said unto him," &c.

Mark i. 29—31.

This Evangelist places the

Luke iv. 38—41.

This Evangelist places the

---

[1] " If," it has been asked, " the command was given at this early date to baptize disciples of ' all nations,' why were the apostles so backward in acting on it, and why does S. Paul so constantly speak of the admission of the Gentiles as τὸ μυστήριον, and as specially revealed to him ? " See Ephes. iii. 3.

healing of Peter's wife's mother after the calling of Peter to be a disciple.

So also with the casting out of a devil in the Synagogue at Capernaum; Mark i. 21—28 compared with Luke iv. 33—37.

healing first and the calling second.

Mark ii. 10. "That ye may know that the Son of man *hath power on earth to forgive sins.*" . .

ii. 28. "The Son of man *is Lord even of the sabbath.*"

Both these statements are made publicly; the former to "certain of the scribes," the latter to the Pharisees.

Mark xiv. 58. "We heard him say, I will destroy this temple that is made with hands, and in three days I will build another made without hands."

That he had claimed the power to forgive sins and to over-rule the observance of the sabbath, would have been a more definite and therefore a more telling charge than the vague words concerning the temple which were ultimately with difficulty and hesitation quoted against him. It is reasonable to infer that the claims were never really made.

Mark iv. 11. "And he said unto them, Unto you is given the mystery of the kingdom

That this should have been deliberately said after the

of God : but unto them that are without, all things are done in parables : that seeing they may see, and not perceive ; and hearing they may hear, and not understand ; lest haply they should turn again, and it should be forgiven them."

first "parable of the Kingdom"—the parable of the Sower—addressed to " a very great multitude," is incredible. How are we to reconcile the hard words with such passages as, " The poor have the gospel preached unto them ;" " In secret have I said nothing ?" Matt. xi. 5. John xviii. 20.

Mark iv. 41. "And they said one to another, *Who then is this*, that even the wind and the sea obey him ?" Cf. Matt. viii. 27, " *What manner of man* (ποταπός) *is this ?*"

Could this question come from men who had already heard of the witness of John the Baptist and had themselves borne witness to the Messiahship of Christ ?

John i. 34. (John the Baptist) " I have seen, *and have borne witness* that this is the Son of God."

41. (Andrew) " *We have found* the Messiah."

45. (Philip). " *We have found him*, of whom Moses in the law, and the prophets did write."

49. (Nathanael) " Thou art the Son of God."

Mark x. 34. "They shall mock him, and shall spit upon him, and shall scourge him and shall kill him." Cf. viii. 31. ix. 31.

Luke xxiv. 25. " And he said unto them, O foolish men, and slow of heart to believe in all that *the prophets* have spoken." Cf. John xii. 16, " These things understood not his disciples at the first : but when Jesus was glorified, then remembered they that these things *were written* of him ;" Luke xviii. 34, "And they understood none of these things ; and this saying was hid from them."

There is first a thrice repeated prediction of the particular events of the Passion ; notwithstanding the precision and the repetition, the prediction is not only not understood but, apparently, not even remembered ; enlightenment comes at last, not from a recollection of the Master's words, but from reference to a passage in Isaiah expressed in much vaguer language and never before applied to Messiah. It is difficult not to believe that the true order is, first, the explanation of Messiah's unlooked for death by written prophecy ; then, the proof of the voluntariness of his death by the testimony of warnings which he must surely have spoken ; and, lastly, the justification of the surprise and perplexity of the disciples at that death by the suggestion that the meaning of those clear and specific warnings had never really been understood.

Mark xi. 12—17.

This Evangelist relates the cleansing of the temple as taking place on the Monday in the holy week.

Matt. xxi. 12 (cf. Luke xix. 45.)

According to the First and Second Evangelists the temple is cleansed on the day of the triumphal entry—Palm-Sunday.

Mark xii. 19. " Master, Moses wrote unto us, If a man's brother die," &c. Cf. x. 3, Matt. xix. 8, xxii. 24. Luke xx. 28.

The passages to which reference is made are Deut. xxiv. 1, xxv. 5.[1]

Mark xii. 26. " As touching the dead, that they are raised ; have ye not read in the book of Moses. . . . how God spake unto him, saying, I am the God of Abraham, and the God of Isaac, and the

The words from Exodus suggest nothing either way, and the inference drawn from them would be as inconclusive to a Pharisee who held,

[1] "Reluctantly the present writer makes the admission which the facts extort from him : he does not see how the Mosaic authorship of Deuteronomy can be maintained ;" Driver, *Critical Notes*, 1887, p. 5. The Professor allows that the laws which the author incorporated were, for the most part, ancient, but, "It is an ideal Moses," he adds, " whose aspirations and aims he unfolds before us."

God of Jacob." Cf. Matt. xxii. 31, Luke xx. 37.

as to a Sadducee who denied, the doctrine of the resurrection. S. Paul is not slow to make use of Jewish Scripture in support of Christian doctrine, but he adduces no such argument for the future state. He knew that the belief of his countrymen, such as it was, in a life to come, rested on the Oral, and not on the Written, Law. The passage, as it stands, looks like an attempt by an unpractised hand to introduce a controversy which should put the Sadducees to silence immediately after the defeat of the Pharisees and Herodians.

Mark xiii. 32. "But of that day or that hour knoweth no one, not even the angels in heaven, neither the Son, but the Father."

Apologists in every age have resorted to the most extraordinary devices to explain these words, *i.e.*, to explain the co-existence of knowledge and ignorance in the person of Christ. The modern argument is that the superhuman knowledge which could discern the inmost thoughts of the disciples,[1] could see even the coin in the mouth of the uncaught fish,[2] could confidently predict the overthrow of Capernaum,[3] of Jerusalem,[4] of the temple,[5] was limited as to one point in one particular event. When we remember that the date of the day of judgment was the pressing question of the sub-apostolic age, and that the question was too precise to be conveniently answered, we have no difficulty in accounting for this one alleged exception.

Mark xiv. 21. " Woe unto that man through whom the Son of man is betrayed ! good were it for that man if he had not been born."

John xiii. 27. "Jesus therefore saith unto him, That thou doest, do quickly." Cf. *v.* 11, " He knew him that should betray him."

Is it conceivable that, with this knowledge, and with the power to use it mercifully, he

[1] Luke ix. 47.   John i. 48; ii. 24, 25; iv. 18; vi. 64; xiii. 11; xvi. 30; xxi. 17.
[2] Matt. xvii. 27, cf. xxi. 2.   [3] Matt. xi. 23.   [4] Luke xxi. 20.
[5] Mark xiii. 2.

O

should have pronounced the traitor's awful doom and then have uttered words which sound like a confirmation of his treachery ?

Moreover, if, according to the First Evangelist (xxvi. 25), the name of the traitor was disclosed to all generally, or, according to the Fourth Evangelist (xiii. 24, 25), to two particularly, how are we to explain the unconcern and inaction of the loyal eleven ? Where was ardent Peter's sword ? The details of the whole story—the indirect distressing charge, the whispered question, the confided secret, the deliberate use of an act of sacred fellowship (the passing of the sop) as a means of private signalling, or, on the other view, the open indication which no one understands, the formal execration which no one deprecates, the explicit exposure of a design which no one attempts to frustrate—all make up a scene which in profane history would excite incredulity and contempt. We have here a curious example of the extent to which long familiarity with unquestioned horrors may quell the protests of reason and deaden the moral sense.

Mark xv. 23. " And they offered him wine mingled with *myrrh*."

[A cup thus prepared was sometimes given as an opiate at a public execution.]

Matt. xxvii. 34. "They gave him wine to drink mingled with *gall*."

Χολή may perhaps stand for a bitter ingredient of any kind, but it seems rather like an application of Ps. lxix. 21, in which passage the bitterness is an aggravation, not an abatement, of pain.

Mark xvi. 9—20.

It is now agreed that these verses, though of undoubted antiquity, did not come from the hand of this writer. In the same way John vii. 53—viii. 11, though no part of the Fourth Gospel, may be a true account dating back to the Apostolic age.

o 2

Luke i. 32. [Gabriel to Mary] "And the Lord God shall give unto him *the throne of his father David :*[1] and he shall reign over *the house of Jacob.*"

Luke i. 52. [Mary] " He hath put down *princes* from their *thrones.*"

Luke i. 71. [Zacharias] "That we should be saved from our *enemies*, and from the hand of all that *hate* us." Cf. Luke ii. 25, [Simeon] "Looking for the *consolation* of Israel ;" Luke ii. 38, [Anna] "And spake of him to all them that were looking for the *redemption* of *Jerusalem.*"

If these were *bonâ fide* predictions, they were never fulfilled. If they are only pious words placed in the mouths of Gabriel, Mary, and Zacharias, then they simply reflect the hopes of Hebrew Christians in a later age that even now, at his approaching second coming, Christ would "restore the kingdom to Israel," and deliver their country from its oppressors.

Luke i. 35. [Gabriel to Mary] "That which is to be born shall be called holy, the Son of God."

Luke ii. 33. " His father *and his mother* were *marvelling* at the things which were spoken concerning him " (by Simeon).

Luke ii. 49, 50. "And he said unto them, How is it that ye sought me ? *Wist ye not* that I must be in my Father's house ? And they *understood not* the saying which he spake unto them."

Mark iii. 21. "And when

---

[1] To explain this relationship it is assumed that Mary was of the lineage of David. But see Appendix III. ii.

his *friends* (cf. *v.* 31) heard it, they went out to lay hold on him : for they said, He is beside himself."

Matt. xiii. 57. " But Jesus said unto them, A prophet is not without honour, save in his own country, and *in his own house.*"

John vii. 5. " For even his *brethren* did not believe on him."

Luke i. 43. [The mother of John the Baptist] " And whence is this to me, that the mother of my Lord should come unto me ?"

John i. 33. [The Baptist] " And *I knew him not.*"

Luke ii. 11. [The angel to the shepherds] " There is born to you this day in the city of David a Saviour, which is Christ the Lord."

,, 17, 18. " And when they saw it they made known concerning the saying which was spoken to them about this child. And all that heard it wondered at the things which were spoken unto them by the shepherds."

Luke iii. 15. " All men reasoned in their hearts concerning *John,* whether haply *he* were the Christ."

There is no hint or trace of the survival of the shepherds' story and of the effect which it produced. What, then, was the intention, and what the result, of the angel's announcement thirty years before ?

Luke ii. 33. "And *his father* and his mother were marvelling at the things which were spoken concerning him."

So the words stand in the Greek in ℵ, B, the oldest extant MSS. In later MSS, 'Joseph' has been substituted for 'his father' and appears in the Authorised Version of the English Bible. In verse 43, a similar alteration was made—'Joseph and his mother' for 'his parents.' [It is fair, however, to say that in *v.* 41 'his parents' has been allowed to stand.] If the correction was due to doctrinal bias, it is difficult not to suspect that the text has been tampered with in other places. Cf. Acts xx. 28. 1 John v. 7, 8. 1 Tim. iii. 16. Coloss. ii. 2. Matt. vi. 13. in illustration.

Luke ii. 39. "And when they had accomplished all things that were according to the law of the Lord (see 22 —24) they returned into Galilee, to their own city Nazareth."

Matt. ii. 16. "Then Herod, when he saw that he was mocked of the wise men . . . . sent forth, and slew all the male children that were in Bethlehem . . . . from *two years* old and under, *according to the time* which he had carefully learned of the wise men."

The first narrative implies a return to Galilee soon after the forty days of purification are over. The second suggests long continued residence in Bethlehem. Moreover, it is difficult not to gather from Matt. ii. 1, 11, 22, 23, that, in the First Gospel, Joseph's home is at Bethlehem. It is curious to note how one Evangelist supplies a train of circumstances to account for the change of scene from Nazareth to Bethlehem, and the other a train of circumstances to explain the change of scene from Bethlehem to Nazareth.

Luke ii. 52. "And Jesus advanced in wisdom."

John vi. 64. "Jesus knew from the beginning who they were that believed not, and who it was that should betray him." Cf. i. 48; ii. 24, 25; iv. 18.

Luke ii. 40. "Filled with wisdom."

John i. 14. "Full of grace and truth."

" He might have possessed an infused knowledge of all truth, and yet have mastered what he already possessed by experience and in detail, in order to satisfy the intellectual conditions of our human existence."[1] Is this explanation even intelligible ? And when Jesus, naturally enough, after the manner of his time, erroneously quotes from the Old Testament, as authentic, passages which are now allowed to be non-authentic, is this an instance of "infused knowledge" unmastered "by experience and in detail ?"

Luke iv. 14—32.

Matt. xiii. 54—58 ; Mark vi. 1—6.

The accounts given of the preaching in the synagogue at Nazareth are hopelessly entangled. The writer of the Third Gospel places it at the beginning of the ministry in Galilee, with an awkward reference to works already done

[1] Liddon, *Bampton Lectures*, Lect. viii.

at Capernaum, and an unsupported narration of an attempt on the preacher's life, whilst the First and Second Evangelists give a much later date.

Luke ix. 7. " And he " (Herod) " was much perplexed, *because that it was said by some* that John was risen from the dead ; and by *some*, that Elijah had appeared ; and by *others*, that one of the old prophets was risen again."

Mark vi. 16. " *But Herod said*, John, whom I beheaded, he is risen." Cf. Matt. xiv. 2.

Here are three groups of persons ready to account for the earthly existence of Christ by a gratuitous theory of resurrection in three different forms. Thus the train is laid for the acceptance of the later legend of his resurrection after death.

Luke ix. 54, 55. [Non-reception of Jesus by Samaritans.] " And when his disciples James and John saw this, they said, Lord, wilt thou that we bid fire to come

Matt. x. 14, 15. [Non-reception of apostles.] " And whosoever shall not receive you, nor hear your words, as ye go forth out of that house or that city, shake off the

down from heaven, and consume them? But he turned and *rebuked* them."

dust of your feet. Verily I say unto you, It shall be *more tolerable* for the land of Sodom and Gomorrah in the day of judgement, *than for that city.*

Luke x. 1. "Now after these things the Lord appointed seventy others, and sent them two and two before his face into every city and place, whither he himself was about to come."

This writer alone relates the appointment of the Seventy. The intention is obvious. It was a fancy of the Jews that the nations of the world were seventy in number. The approach to Samaria on the final journey to Jerusalem (ix. 51, 52), in connection with the charge to the Twelve (Matt. x. 5.) not to go "into any way of the Gentiles," and not to enter "into any city of the Samaritans," suggests the thought of a special mission which would be full of consolation to heathen readers. The point is further enforced by a parable (x. 30—35) and a miracle (xvii. 16) in which Samaritans are presented in a favourable light. The charge to the Seventy is substantially the same as that given to the Twelve in the preceding chapter, ix. 1—5.

The whole narrative is an allegorical presentation of the later extension of the preaching of the Kingdom. The writer is a Gentile writing for Gentiles.

Luke xi. 1.

In this Gospel the Lord's Prayer has a distinct historical setting and is called forth by a special circumstance.

Matt vi. 9.

In the First Gospel the Lord's Prayer is given in the course of the Sermon on the Mount.

Luke xi. 39—52.

Matt. xxiii. 1—39.

The denunciation of the Scribes and Pharisees, according to the Third Evangelist, takes place at a meal in a Pharisee's house and the circumstances under which it was spoken are minutely described. In the First Gospel it forms part of a discourse in the Temple on the Tuesday in the holy week.

Luke xi. 51. " From the blood of Abel unto the blood of Zachariah."

Gen. iv. 10.

Both are evidently regarded as historic persons. Is this one of those 'mythical' parts of Genesis " in which we cannot distinguish the historical germ ?" (*Lux Mundi*, 357, 10th ed.) The same question may be asked with regard to the references in Luke iv. 26, xvii. 26, 29, 32, xx. 27, 37, John iii. 14, vi. 49, vii. 22.

Luke xii. 1—12, 22—59.

Passages from the sixth, tenth and twenty-fourth chapters of the First Gospel are here thrown into one continuous discourse, with definite marks of time and of historical connection. We are driven to the conclusion, either that the sayings were under different circumstances repeated word for word, or that this writer invented occasions for introducing them.

For other instances of historical setting in the Third Gospel not in agreement with the historical connection of the First and Second, see ii. 39, iv. 16, 31—36, v. 1—11, vi. 17, 27, 35, vii. 36—50 (?), viii. 19, x. 2, 4, &c., 13, 22, xi. 33, 37—52, xiii. 18, 19, 20, 21, 28, 29, xiv. 11, 16— 24, xv. 4—7, xvii. 2, 3, 4, 23—37, xviii. 14, 35, xix. 11 —27, xxii. 21, 25, 26, xxiii. 36—37 (?).

Luke xiii. 34. "O Jerusalem, Jerusalem which killeth the prophets. . . . how often would I have gathered thy children together, even as a hen gathereth her own brood under her wings, and ye would not !"

Matt xxiii. 37.

The lamentation over Jerusalem, introduced amongst the incidents of a journey to Jerusalem by the Third Evangelist, is placed at the close of the last address in the Temple by the First Evangelist.

Luke xvi. 16. "The law and the prophets were *until John :* from that time the gospel of the kingdom of God is preached."

Luke xvi. 17. "But it is easier for heaven and earth to pass away, than for one tittle of the law to fall."

Luke xviii. 7. "Shall not God avenge his elect, which cry to him day and night ?" Cf. Matt. xxiv. 22, 24, 31 ; Mark xiii. 20, 22, 27.

These seven passages in which the 'elect' are spoken of seem hardly to belong to the original sayings of Christ.

They do not fall in with his generally sanguine view of the Kingdom, and they appear rather to express the failing hope of a later age under the pressure of persecution. Compare also the language of vi. 22 ; xii. 11 ; xxi. 12, 24.

Luke xx. 28. " Moses wrote unto us." Cf. Mark xii. 19 ; John i. 45 ; v. 46.

(Deut. xxv. 5 ; xviii. 15, 18.)

" To suppose that Moses could have written a book in Hebrew, and with a Semitic alphabet, would be to antedate the writing of books by nearly 1000 years, and the employment of alphabetic writing in general by more than 500 years." Prof. Max Müller, *Gifford Lectures*.

Luke xxii. 18. " I say unto you, I will not drink from henceforth of the fruit of the vine, until the kingdom of God shall come."

Luke xxiv. 30. Cf. Acts i. 4 ; x. 41.

Luke xxiii. 5. [The chief priests to Pilate] "He stirreth up the people, teaching throughout all Judæa, and *beginning from Galilee even unto this place.*"

Cf. Acts x. 36, 37. [Peter to Cornelius] "The word. . . which was published throughout all Judæa, *beginning from Galilee.*"

The preaching of the Gospel begins in Galilee and in course of time reaches Judæa.

John ii. 1—v. 47.

According to this writer there was, before the Galilæan ministry recorded by the other Evangelists (Matt. iv. 12, Mark i. 14, Luke iv. 14), an early ministry in Judæa of several months, and accompanied by miracles, public preaching, and open conflict with the Jews. (See ii. 15, 18, 19, 23, v. 8, 17—47). Two visits to Galilee, it is true, are mentioned, but they are singularly brief, are quickly passed over, are expressly connected with only two "signs," and are apparently unattended by any public preaching. In the sixth chapter the Galilæan ministry begins, but the "published word" has its home in Judæa and spreads itself northwards. And yet the harmonists ask us to believe that when Jesus "from that time *began to preach*" (Matt. iv. 17) he had already completed a fully developed and widely published ministry of at least nine months in Judœa.

Luke xxiv. 6, 7, 8. "He is not here, but is risen : remember how he spake unto you when he was yet in Galilee, saying that the Son of man must be delivered up. . . . . and the third day rise again. *And they* ("the women" from Galilee, of whom Mary Magdalene was one) "*remembered his words.*"

John xx. 2, 15. "She" (Mary Magdalene) "runneth therefore, and cometh to Simon Peter. . . . and saith unto them, *They have taken away* the Lord out of the tomb, and we know not where they have laid him."

"Sir, if *thou hast borne him hence,* tell me where thou hast laid him, and I will take him away."

John i. 1. "The Word was God."

John x. 36. "Whom the Father *sanctified* (or consecrated) and sent into the world."

xvii. 3. "This is life eternal, that they should know *thee the only true God,* and him whom thou didst send, even Jesus Christ."

xvii. 21. "That they may all be one ; *even as* thou, Father, art in me, and I in thee, *that they also* may be in us."

xiv. 28. "The Father is greater than I."

xvii. 24. "That they may behold my glory, which *thou hast given* me."

vii. 29. "I am *from him,* and he sent me."

John i. 15—36.

According to the statements here made, the Baptist must have possessed a discernment of the nature, dignity and office of Christ, and a conception of his kingdom, far exceeding those of even the apostles themselves. Cf. Acts i. 3.

Matt. xi. 11. "He that is but little in the kingdom of heaven is greater than he" (John the Baptist).

John i. 15, 29, 33, 36. "John beareth witness of him . . . saying, He that cometh after me is become before me : for he was before me." "And he looked upon Jesus as he walked, and saith, Behold, the Lamb of God !" (Cf. Luke iii. 22.) "On the morrow he seeth Jesus coming unto him and saith, "Behold the Lamb of God, which taketh away the sin of the world." "He that sent me to baptize with water, he said unto me, Upon whomsoever thou shalt see the spirit descending, and abiding upon him, the same is he that baptizeth with the Holy Spirit." Cf. John iii. 25—30.

Here the Pre-existence, Messiahship, and Mediatorial

Matt. xi. 2, 3. "Now when John heard in the prison the works of the Christ, he sent by his disciples and said unto him, Art thou he that cometh, or look we for another ?"

Here there is further inquiry and a desire for fuller information.

Moreover, it would seem from comparison of these verses with John iii. 25, Acts xviii. 25, xix. 2, 3, that, contrary to what might have been expected, the Baptist did not disband his disciples, that these with their converts formed a distinct, if not an unfriendly, body,

P

Office of Jesus are unhesitatingly acknowledged and affirmed.

and that, so far from handing down the testimony of the Holy Spirit received from their master, they are found not even to have heard from him that there was any Holy Spirit.

John i. 20. [In answer to *Priests and Levites* sent to John the Baptist by the *Pharisees*, probably from the Sanhedrin, with an official inquiry], "And he confessed and denied not ; and he confessed, I am not the Christ."

Matt. ii. 4. "And gathering together all the *chief priests and scribes* of the people, he inquired of them where the Christ should be born. And they said unto him, *In Bethlehem of Judæa.*"

How then could the question, whether *ho* were the Christ, be put by the same learned authorities to the Baptist, whose birthplace, as was well known, was not Bethlehem ?

John i. 29—ii. 1.

The distinct notes of time given in these verses leave no room for the insertion of the forty days of the Temptation.

Matt. iv. 1, 2.

John ii. 19. "Jesus answered and said unto them,

Mark xiv. 57, 58. "And there stood up certain, and

Destroy this temple, and in three. days I will raise it up."

bare false witness against him, saying, We heard him say, I will destroy this temple that is made with hands, and in three days I will build another made without hands." Cf. Matt. xxvi. 60.

John ii. 19, 21. " Destroy this temple, and in three days I will raise *it* up. . . . But he spake of the temple of his body."[1]

Mark xiv. 58. " We heard him say, I will destroy this temple that is made with hands, and in three days I will build *another* made without hands."

Here the word " another " gives a different character to the sentence and demands for it a different interpretation.

John iii. 5. "Jesus answered, Verily, verily, I say unto thee, " Except a man be born *of water and the Spirit*, he cannot enter into the kingdom of God."

John i. 33. " He that sent me to baptize *with water*, he said unto me, Upon whomsoever thou shalt see the Spirit

John iii. 23. " And John also was baptising in Ænon . . . . . and they came, and were baptized." Cf. Matt. iii. 11.

Therefore the Baptist, after testifying to the superior baptism which was to supersede his own, continues to receive

[1] " The term 'temple' is not applicable, and is nowhere else applied, to Christ's natural body. His 'body' in N.T. language is his Church ;" *Schenkel.*

descending, and abiding upon him, the same is he that baptizeth *with the Holy Spirit.*"

John iii. 22. " After these things came Jesus and his disciples into the land of Judæa ; and there he tarried with them and baptized " (cf. iv. 2) necessarily, according to iii. 5, with water *and the Spirit.*

candidates for the inferior baptism with water only, although Jesus himself was baptizing close at hand.

John iii. 13, 14. " And no man hath ascended into heaven, but he that descended out of heaven, even the Son of man, which is in heaven. And as Moses lifted up the serpent in the wilderness, even so must the Son of man be lifted up." Cf. viii. 28 ; xii. 32.

These words were either actually spoken by Jesus to Nicodemus at a very early date, or they give the reflections of the Evangelist after the event. In Matt. xvi. 21 it is said that at the *end* of his ministry Jesus " *began* " to predict the later events of his life.

John iii. 22, 23. " After these things came Jesus and his disciples into the land of Judæa ; and there he tarried with them and baptized. And *John also was baptizing* in Ænon."

Here the preaching of Jesus and the calling of disciples

Matt. iv. 12, 17. " Now when he heard that *John was delivered up,* he withdrew into Galilee . . . . . From that time *began Jesus to preach,* and to say, Repent ye ; for the kingdom of heaven is at hand." See also 18—22.

precede the imprisonment of John.

By this Evangelist the beginning of the ministry and the call of the first disciples are placed after the arrest of the Baptist.

John iv. 41, 42. "And many more (Samaritans) believed because of his word; and they said . . . . . we know that this is indeed the *Saviour of the world.*"

Is this " magnificent conception of the work of Christ," in such a place and at such a time, historically conceivable ?

John iv. 25. " The woman saith unto him, I know that *Messiah* cometh."

John iv. 43, 44. "And after the two days he went forth from thence into Galilee. *For* Jesus himself testified, that a prophet hath no honour in his own country. So when he came into Galilee, the Galilæans received him."

Mark vi. 4. Matt. xiii. 57. Luke iv. 24.

In the Synoptic Gospels "his own country" is Galilee, in the Fourth Gospel it is Judæa. But compare John i. 45, 46, vii. 41, 42, 52.

John v. 18. " For this cause therefore the Jews sought the more to kill him, because he not only brake the sabbath, but also called

Matt. xvi. 16. "And Simon Peter answered and said, Thou art the Christ, the Son of the living God."

John x. 35—36. " If he

God his own Father, *making himself equal with God.*"

called them *gods,* unto whom the word of God came . ... . say ye of him, whom the Father *sanctified and sent* into the world, Thou blasphemest ; because I said I am the Son of God ?" Cf. *v.* 30.

The title Son of God as an appellation of the Messiah could not at that time have carried any notion of equality with God. The metaphysical sense of the term, with the thought of "eternal, continuous generation," is of much later date, the time of Origen.

John v. 18. " For this cause therefore the Jews sought the more to kill him, because he not only brake the sabbath, but also called God his own Father, *making himself equal with God.*" Cf. x. 33.

[The ἴδιον of *v.* 18 is thrown in by objectors and is not justified by anything in the statement of *v.* 17 as it stands.]

John i. 49. " Nathanael answered him, Rabbi, thou art the Son of God ; thou art *King of Israel.*" Cf. i. 34 ; xi. 27 ; ix. 35, 37.

If the Baptist, Nathanael, Martha, and Jesus himself could use the title 'Son of God' as simply synonymous with Messiah, how could " the Jews" understand, or pretend to understand, by the use of the name any assertion of equality with God ?

John v. 46. " He (Moses) wrote of me."

Deut. xviii. 15—18. (Cf. Acts iii. 22 ; vii. 37.)

"We may suppose Deuteronomy to be a republication of the law in the spirit and power of Moses, put dramatically in his mouth ;" *Lux Mundi*, p. 355 (ed. 10).

Similarly Prof. Driver (*Introd. to Lit. of O. T.* p. 82) says that the composition of this Book is probably "not later than the reign of Manasseh." Again (p. 84), "the true author is the writer who introduces Moses in the third person."

John vi. 70. "Jesus answered them, Did not I choose you the twelve, and one of you is a devil ?"

This is supposed to have been said a year before the last visit to Jerusalem.

Matt. xix. 28. "And Jesus said unto them, Verily I say unto you, that ye which have followed me, in the regeneration when the Son of man shall sit on the throne of his glory, ye also *shall sit upon twelve thrones*, judging the twelve tribes of Israel."

This is said at a much later date, and apparently the idea of the fall of one of the Twelve has not yet presented itself. Cf. xxvi. 21.

John vii. 52. [The Sanhedrin to Nicodemus.] "Search, and see that out of Galilee ariseth no prophet."

A statement so inaccurate could hardly have been made by a body so learned. Jonah, Hosea, Nahum (and perhaps Elijah, Elisha, and Amos) were of Galilee.

John x. 8. "All that came before me are thieves and robbers."

Matt. xxiii. 2. The *scribes* and the *Pharisees* sit on Moses' seat. All things therefore whatsoever they bid you, these do and observe."

Luke xiii. 28. . . . . . "When ye shall see Abraham, and Isaac, and Jacob, and *all the prophets,* in the kingdom of God." . . . .

John xii. 1, 2. "Jesus therefore *six* days before the passover came to Bethany. . . . So they made him a supper there."

Mark xiv. 1—3. "Now after *two* days was the feast of the passover. . . . . And while he was in Bethany in the house of Simon the leper, as he sat at meat." . . . Cf. Matt. xxvi. 6.

John xii. 6. "Now this he said, not because he cared for the poor ; but because he was a thief, and having the bag took away what was put therein."

Matt. xxvi. 8. " When *the disciples* saw it, they had indignation, saying, To what purpose is this waste ?"

Mark xiv. 4. "There were *some* that had indignation

This passage marks the growth of the Judas legend. The desire to connect the "indignation" only with one hated name, and the charge of dishonesty, are in striking contrast to the more generous statements of the Synoptists.

With the support of ii. 25; vi. 64, 70, 71, we are tempted also to ask why one known as a thief and foreknown as a traitor was retained in a position of trust and familiarity.

among themselves, saying, To what purpose hath this waste of the ointment been made?"

John xiii. 38. Cf. Luke xxii. 34.

According to these two Evangelists the prediction of Peter's denial takes place during the Supper.

Matt. xxvi. 34. Cf. Mark xiv. 30.

These writers place the prediction on the road to Gethsemane.

John xv. 15. "All things that I heard from my Father I have made known unto you."

Here a full and direct revelation from the Father is

Luke xxiv. 27. "And beginning from Moses and from all the prophets, he interpreted to them in all the scriptures the things concerning himself."

What need would there be

spoken of as given before the Resurrection.

of weaker and remoter proof by argument after the Resurrection ?

John xvii. 12. "Not one of them perished, but the son of perdition ; that the scripture might be fulfilled."

These words have all the appearance of an *ex post facto* comment upon the traitor's death ; but they are here made to form part of the Master's prayer for his disciples whilst Judas is still alive.

John xvii. 18. "As thou didst send me into the world, even so *sent I them* into the world."

John xx. 21. "As the Father hath sent me, even so *send I you.*"

The Evangelist, confusing for the moment his own historical stand-point with that of the speaker, makes the prayer for those who had been *sent* precede the actual *sending.*

Similar instances of the effect of subsequent history on the composition of this last discourse may be found in xv. 6, 15, xvi. 2, xvii. 20. See also iv. 21—24, 38, x. 16, xii. 21.

John xviii. 17. Cf. 25, 27.

Peter's denials take place in the house of Annas.

John xviii. 24. " Annas therefore sent him bound unto Caiaphas the high priest."

Matt. xxvi. 57, 70, 72, 74.

Here the scene is laid in the house of Caiaphas.

The balance of MSS. readings is in favour of ὅυν, "therefore." The verse, then, must stand where it is placed in the text and must not be inserted into *v.* 15. It can only introduce for the first time a fresh incident. If this be so, the interview described in verses 15—23 is supposed by the writer to have been held before Annas "the high priest." But the first three Evangelists know nothing of this interview, and by the term "the high priest" they mean Caiaphas to whom alone the title belonged.

John xviii. 28. " And they themselves entered not into the palace, that they might not be defiled, *but might eat the passover.*"[1] (Cf. xiii. 1, 29, and perhaps xix. 36).

Mark xiv. 12. (Matt. xxvi. 17. Luke xxii. 7). " On the first day of unleavened bread, *when they sacrificed the passover*, his disciples say unto him, Where wilt thou that

---

[1] It has been contended, however, that τὸ πάσχα here refers, not to the Paschal Lamb, but to the *Chagigah*, another sacrifice of the Paschal feast, which was brought on Nisan 15. See Edersheim,

From this passage it is clear that by this writer the crucifixion is placed *before* the eating of the Passover— in other words, in the afternoon of the 14th Nisan.

we go and make ready that thou mayest eat the passover ?"

From this passage it is equally clear that the Synoptists place the crucifixion *after* the Passover—in other words in the afternoon of the 15th Nisan.[2] If we adhere to the day of the week, Friday, the difference of a day in the date of the month involves, of course, a difference of twelve months in the date of the year.

John xix. 14. "It was about the *sixth* hour"—*i.e.*, twelve o'clock in the day.

If it be argued that some special mode of reckoning time has been followed by this writer, and that he means six a.m., space will have to be found between the early morning (πρωί) and six o'clock

Mark xv. 25. "And it was the *third* hour, and they crucified him "—*i.e.*, nine a.m.

Mark xv. 33. "And when the sixth hour was come, there was *darkness over the whole land* until the ninth hour."

Life and Times of the Messiah, vol. ii. Of this extension there is no evidence, says Dean Plumptre.

[2] This is done, apparently, in order to identify the Last Supper with the eating of the Paschal meal and so to give it the character of a Passover.

for the three scenes of the trial before Pilate, for the sending to Herod and the setting at nought by his soldiers, and for the final scourging and mockery before the delivery for crucifixion ; (John xviii. 28—xix. 14 and Luke xxiii. 6—12). In ch. iv. 6. "the sixth hour" can hardly be anything but noon,[1] and this would require the ordinary Roman and Jewish reckoning of time, and the same reckoning here would make twelve o'clock the hour of the delivery. Compare also i. 39, iv. 52, for similar notes of time.

John xx. 28. " Thomas answered and said unto him, My Lord and my God."	John xx. 17. "Go unto my brethren, and say to them, I ascend unto . . . . . *my God and your God.*"

[1] So late an hour as six in the evening, with an Eastern twilight, is excluded by the length of the conversation which follows and by the force of verses 16 and 35. Dr. Sanday (*Expositor*, Jan. 1892) after a careful study of the evidence, and especially of Bilfinger's exhaustive treatises on the subject, confesses that he is obliged to pronounce against the reckoning from midnight to midday defended by Tholuck and Wieseler and adopted by Bp. Westcott (*St. John*, p. 282).

John xx. 28. ".Thomas answered and said unto him, My Lord and my God."

This is said in the presence of the Ten who had already been convinced. Cf. *v.* 20.

Matt. xxviii. 16. " But the eleven disciples went into Galilee. . . . And when they saw him, they worshipped him : *but some doubted.*"

Some, therefore, doubted in Galilee who had already been persuaded beyond all doubt in Jerusalem. If it is contended that those who doubted were. unmentioned bystanders, or inferior disciples, then there is nothing to limit the Commission given in *vv.* 19, 20, to the Eleven.

John xxi. 1—14.

The miraculous draught of fishes.

Luke v. 1—11.

No miraculous draught of fishes is recorded by the First and Second Evangelists in the corresponding sections (Matt. iv. 18—22. Mark i. 16—20). The narratives in the Third and Fourth Gospels are so closely similar that we can only suppose that each writer has given to the same tradition his own historic setting. But, if this be so, what becomes of the history?

APPENDIX III.

THE CHRISTOLOGY OF THE NEW TESTAMENT.

AUTHORITIES.—Dorner, *Entwickelungsgeschichte der Lehre von der Person Christi*, 1845 ; Beyschlag, *Die Christologie des Neuen Testaments*, 1866 ; Réville, *Histoire du Dogme de la divinité de Jésus-Christ*, 1876 ; Gess, *Christi Person und Werk*, 1887 ; Harnack, *Dogmengeschichte*, 1888—90 ; Liddon, *Bampton Lecture*, 1866 ; Reuss, *Histoire de la Théologie Chrétienne*, 1864 ; Stap, *Études historiques et critiques sur les origines du Christianisme*, 1891.

It will be convenient for our purpose to take the Books of the New Testament in three groups ; (1) the Pauline and Deutero-Pauline Epistles, the Epistles of Peter, James and Jude, and the Epistle to the Hebrews ; (2) the Synoptists and the Acts of the Apostles ; (3) the Johannine Writings.

The two Epistles to the Corinthians, the Epistle to the Galatians, and the Epistle to the Romans are generally allowed to be undoubtedly genuine.[1]

[1] The genuineness even of these is questioned by the newer school of Steck, Loman and Völter.

There is a strong probability in favour of the Epistles to the Thessalonians and of the Epistle to the Philippians, and, in a less degree, in favour of the Epistles to the Colossians and to Philemon; there is more doubt as to the Epistle to the Ephesians; and doubt becomes almost certain denial in the case of the so-called Pastoral Epistles.

One reason for the hesitation felt with regard to nine out of the thirteen Epistles lies in the fact that the Christology of those which are questioned differs in a marked degree from that of those which are admitted to be genuine. It is, indeed, conceivable that in course of time the Apostle may have expanded his conception of the Person of Christ, and may have expressed himself in the bolder tone of the later Epistles. But, however this may be, we shall be wise in taking the four undisputed Epistles by themselves, regarding them as the first documentary evidence open to us as to the belief of at least one prominent Christian teacher in the Apostolic age with respect to the nature of Christ.

I. The Pauline Epistles.

i.—Rom. 1 Cor. 2 Cor. Gal.

The monotheistic basis of the Apostle's belief is very distinctly laid down. From the One God Jesus is carefully distinguished, so carefully that, in the face of this distinction, it is impossible to give to Rom. ix. 5

any other than one of the renderings placed in the margin of the Revised Version.[1]

Rom. iii. 30; xvi. 27. 1 Cor. viii. 4, 6. Gal. iii. 20.

Jesus is :—

The One, Pre-existent, Archetypal, Heavenly Man,[2] (cf. John iii. 13 ; vi. 62. Rom. viii. 29. Ephes. i. 4, 5), the Second Man, the Last Adam; born, according to the flesh, of the seed of David, and afterwards 'determined' to be the Son of God by the Resurrection.[3]

Rom. v. 15. 1 Cor. xv. 21, 45, 47; x. 4, 9. 2 Cor. viii. 9.
Rom. i. 3. Gal. iii. 16; iv. 4. Rom. i. 4.

He is the ' Spirit' of God and he ' became,' when

---

[1] Τὸν γοῦν Ἰησοῦν οὔτε Παῦλος ἐτόλμησεν εἰπεῖν θεόν.—Cyril of Alexandria.

[2] On the ideal pre-existence attributed by Jewish apocryphal writers to the Patriarchs, to Moses, even to the Tabernacle and the Temple, see Harnack, *Dogmengeschichte*, i. 89 ; Schürer, *Geschichte des Judischen Volkes*, II. ii. 29 ; Gfrörer, *Jahrhundert des Heils ;* and cf. Exod. xxv. 9, 40 ; xxvi. 30 ; xxvii. 8. Numb. viii. 4. The spiritual ' heavenly man' is a favourite conception with Philo. Compare also the personification of ' Principalities,' ' Powers,' ' Virtues,' &c., in the tabulated hierarchies of angels current among the Jews.

[3] Cf. Acts xiii. 23 ; xvii. 31 ; where this ' determination ' of Sonship is still more definitely expressed in speeches attributed to S. Paul :—" *Of this man's seed* hath God according to promise brought unto Israel a Saviour, Jesus ;" " He hath appointed a day in the which he will judge the world in righteousness by *the man whom he hath ordained ;* whereof he hath given assurance unto all men, in that he hath raised him from the dead." [There is here not the slightest hint, and apparently not the slightest inkling, of any previous ' assurance' by a miraculous birth.]

Q

raised from the dead, a life-giving spirit, and a bestower of spiritual blessings.

2 Cor. iii. 17. 1 Cor. xv. 45; xii. 27. 2 Cor. iv. 10; xiii. 5.
Rom. i. 7. 1 Cor. i. 3. 2 Cor. i. 2. Gal. i. 3.

To confess that he is Lord is the prime article of Christian belief. But this title he holds by creation and bestowal, and not by original and inseparable right. (Cf. Acts ii. 34—36. Phil. ii. 9—11).

Rom. x. 9. 1 Cor. xii. 3.

He is the 'Image,' εἰκὼν, of God in the 'likeness,' ὁμόιωμα, of flesh. (But the same word 'image' is used of man in relation to God in 1 Cor. xi. 7, and of man in relation to Christ in Rom. viii. 29; Col. iii. 10).

Rom. viii. 3. 2 Cor. iv. 4.

He is the Agent of God's activity in the created world. (The apostle is thinking possibly only of the spiritual world in which the agency of Christ produces the 'new creature;' cf. Gal. vi. 15; Eph. ii. 10, iv. 24; Col. iii. 10).

1 Cor. viii. 6; cf. 1 Cor. i. 30; 2 Cor. v. 18.

But God is his God (cf. especially Eph. i. 17, and John xx. 17; Rev. iii. 2, 12), and Head;

Rom. xv. 6. 2 Cor. i. 3. Eph. i. 3. 2 Cor. xi. 31.
1 Cor. xi. 3; iii. 23.

By Him he is sent;

Rom. viii. 3. Gal. iv. 4.

By Him he is raised from the dead;

Rom. vi. 4; viii. 11. 1 Cor. vi. 14.

By His power he lives;

2 Cor. xiii. 4.

To Him he is therefore subject, and the power which he receives he restores.

1 Cor. iii. 23; xi. 3; xv. 28. 2 Cor. iv. 4, 6.

In relation to men, Jesus is :—

The 'Firstborn'[1] among many brethren, subject with them to weakness and suffering, but 'without sin'.[2]

Rom. viii. 29. 2 Cor. xiii. 4; i. 5; v. 21. Gal. ii. 17.

ii.—1, 2 Thess. Phil. Coloss. Eph. 1, 2 Tim. Tit.

In this group of Epistles Jesus Christ is :—

The 'Beloved of God ;' the 'Son of His love ;' His 'Son.'

Eph. i. 6. Col. i. 13. 1 Thess. i. 10.

Pre-existent ;

Eph. i. 4.; iv. 9, 10. Col. i. 15, 17. Phil. ii. 6.

[1] The Christological meaning of πρωτότοκος in the New Testament must be determined by the four following passages :—Rom. viii. 29 ; Col. i. 15, 18 ; Rev. i. 5. The first and third are explained by the defining power of the prepositions which are used in conjunction. The question remains whether the second 'first-born of all creation,' is analogous to the fourth, 'first-born of the dead '—in a word, whether Christ is one, though the first, of created things, as he is one, though the first raised, of the dead. Grammatically the identity of construction might, perhaps, be maintained, but the context of Col. i. 15, especially *v.* 17, requires us to admit that the intention of the expression is that Christ is *prior* to all creation. Cf. Rev. iii. 14. See, however, Reuss, *Théologie Chrétienne,* II. 75.

The word πρωτότοκος, like ἐικών, is one of the Alexandrian terms applied to the *Logos* under the slightly varied form πρωτόγονος.

[2] The use of ὁμοίωμα above is thereby explained. His humanity was only a 'likeness' of *sinful* flesh. The true 'Heavenly Man'

A 'Form' of God; an 'Image' of God (as in 2 Cor. iv. 4); and 'Firstborn' absolutely (as in Heb i. 6);

Phil. ii. 6. Col i. 15. (But see iii. 10).

It is the good pleasure of God that His 'Fulness' should dwell in him bodily.[1]

Col. i. 19. (But see ii. 10, and Eph. iii. 19).
Col. ii. 9. (But see Eph. i. 22, 23. iv. 12).

Conversely, he is, with the life of the saints, in God; the source and centre, the creative agent and final cause, of the Universe.

Col. iii. 3. (Cf. 1 Cor. iii. 23; i. 16).

By the Father he is :—

Raised from the dead;

Eph. i. 20. 1 Thess. i. 10.

Exalted;

Eph. i. 20. Phil. iii. 21. Col. ii. 9.

Endowed with powers and titles ('Lord,' 'Heir,' 'Head') superior to those already enjoyed, and conferred by way of reward.

Eph. i. 22, 23. (Cf. 1 Cor. xv. 27. Gal. iii. 16, 18).
Col. ii. 9—11. (Cf. Rom. viii. 17). 2 Thess. i. 7—10.

is also the ideal Earthly Man, subject in the flesh to weakness (ii. Cor. xiii. 4), and death (Rom. vi. 9), but preserved by the 'spirit of holiness' (Rom. i. 4) from the taint of sin. Inasmuch as the absence of inward propensity to sin would not be outwardly apparent, the *likeness* of sinful flesh would still remain.

[1] The essential distinction between God and Christ could scarcely be more definitely expressed. The terms 'good pleasure' and 'dwell,' to name no other, mark points of departure in thought and time, and imply the coming to pass of that which had not been a necessary and eternal fact.

But the Father of glory, to Whose glory he is confessed as Lord, is " the God of our Lord Jesus Christ;"

Eph. i. 3, 17.   Phil. ii. 11.   (Cf. Rom. x. 9.   1 Cor. xii. 3).
1 Thess. i. 9—10 ; iv. 14.

To Him alone belong absolute majesty, the will to save and the power to judge.

1 Thess. iii. 13 ; iv. 3.   2 Thess. i. 5.   1 Thess. i. 4, 5, 9.
2 Thess. ii. 13.

In the Pastoral Epistles Christ Jesus is described as :—

The one ' Mediator,' himself man, between the One God and men ; of the seed of David ; risen from the dead ;

1 Tim. ii. 5 ; iii. 16; vi. 15.   2 Tim. ii. 8.

The ' Saviour' who abolished death ;[1]

2 Tim. i. 10; ii. 10.   Tit. i. 4; ii. 13; iii. 6.

Pre-existent ;

2 Tim. i. 9, 10.

The righteous ' Judge' who shall judge the quick and the dead ;

2 Tim. i. 18; iv. 1, 8.

But the time of his ' appearing'_ is known only to " the only God," " Who only hath immortality," " the blessed and only Potentate," " the blessed God."

1 Tim. vi. 14, 15 ; i. 17; vi. 15, 16 ; i. 11.

---

[1] Some have tried to draw argument for the deity of Christ from Tit. i. 3—" according to the commandment of *God our Saviour* "—forgetting that in these Epistles the term Saviour is used nearly as frequently of the Father :—1 Tim. i. 1 ; ii. 3 ; iv. 10.   Tit. ii. 10; iii. 4.   Cf. Luke i. 47.   Jude 25.

iii.—1 Pet. Jas. Jude.

The writer of the First Epistle of Peter, like the Synoptists, knows of no personally pre-existent Christ.[1] He speaks of Him as:—

'Foreknown' in the knowledge of God ; (cf. i. 2, Rom. viii. 29) ; 'Elect' with God ;

1 Pet. i. 20 ; ii. 4, (cf. 6.)

The 'Chief Shepherd' hereafter to be manifested ;

1 Pet. v. 4 ; ii. 25. (Cf. i. 7, 13). Jas. v. 8, 9.

Sinless ;

1 Pet. i. 19 ; ii. 22 ; iii. 18.

Raised by the Father from the dead ; receiving glory from Him on His right hand ; angels being made subject unto him ;

1 Pet. i. 21 ; iii. 22. (2 Pet. i. 17).

---

[1] Two verses in this Epistle—i. 23 and i. 11—have been pressed into argument for the writer's belief in the pre-existence of Christ ; but a comparison of the first with the emphatic repetition in *v.* 25, and the recollection that 'the prophets' of the second passage are most likely 'prophets' of the Apostolic Church (cf. Rom. viii. 9. Gal. iv. 6) who testified beforehand the sufferings *unto,* or for, Christ, will give a very different interpretation of the texts.

Similarly in 2 Pet. i. 1. "Our God and Saviour Jesus Christ" should rather be translated, Our God and the Saviour, both because it is highly improbable that the Epistle would open without mention of the Father, and because the omission of the article in the Greek decides nothing. Cf. Tit. ii. 13. "To speak of the 'appearing' of God the Father," says Usteri commenting on this last passage, "would be against all analogy ;" but the closing words of the so-called Second Epistle of Clement, "we know not the day of God's 'appearing,'" supply at least one instance to the contrary.

Christ, sanctified in the heart as Lord, the Lord of glory ;

1 Pet. iii. 15.   Jas. i. 1 ;   ii. 1.   Jude 4.   (2 Pet. i. 2).

But the Father is the source of all blessing and the ultimate object of belief ;

1 Pet. v. 10 ;   iv. 10, 11, 16, 17, 19 ;   i. 21.

He is the God of Jesus Christ ;

1 Pet. i. 3.   Cf. Jude 25.

iv.—Hebrews.

It is impossible to gather from the Epistle to the Hebrews any consistent theory of the Person of Christ. In the opening verses the title Son of God seems to include not only all that was connected with the conception of Messiah, but also nearly all that attached to the idea of the *Logos*.

The ' Son ' (i. 28 ; iii. 6 ; iv. 14 ; v. 8 ; vi. 6 ; vii. 3, 28 ; x. 29) is :—

The ' Effulgence ' of the glory of God ;

i. 3.

The 'Impress ' of His substance ;

i. 3.

His 'Agent ' in creative action ;

i. 2 ; cf. xi. 3.

He upholds all things by the word of his Father's power ;

i. 3 ; cf. xi. 3.

But the Son is at the same time :—

Man, son of man ;

ii. 6.

Of the tribe of Judah ;
vii. 14.

'Firstborn' among many sons ;
i. 6 ; ii. 10, 11 ; xii. 7, 9, 23.

'Brought' into the world ;[1]
i. 6.

In all things made like unto his fellow-men, sin only excepted ;
ii. 11—14, 17 ; iv. 15 ; vii. 26 ; ix. 14.

He prays and cries with tears to his Father Who is able to save him from death ; by the grace of God tastes death ; and by Him is brought again from the dead.
v. 7 ; ii. 9 ; xiii. 20.

By his God he is :—

'Anointed' ;
i. 9.

Made 'perfect' ;
ii. 10 ; v. 9 ; vii. 28.

Named a 'High Priest' and 'appointed' ;[2]
v. 10 ; iii. 2 ; cf. v. 5.

To do His will he comes ;
x. 7.

To Him he is faithful ;
iii. 2.

[1] The ambiguity of the word 'again' in i. 6. makes it possible that the reference may be to a second Advent.

[2] If this be indeed the meaning of ποιήσαντι, and not rather 'created' him, without reference to any office.

By Him he is heard because of his 'godly fear' (ἐυλάβεια) ;

v. 7.

In His heavenly sanctuary he is a 'Minister'; before His face he 'appears'; to Him he is 'offered'; he is His 'Apostle' ;[1]

viii. 2 ; ix. 24, 28 ; iii. 1.

By Him he is 'counted worthy' of glory; 'crowned' with glory and honour ; 'appointed' heir of all things ;

iii. 3 ; i. 9 ; i. 2.

He glorifies not himself to be 'made' a high priest ;

v. 5.

He 'becomes' better than the angels ;[2] 'becomes' merciful ; 'learns' obedience ;

i. 4 ; ii. 17 ; v. 8.

He even becomes Son of God, for the name is one which he 'inherits,' and it dates from a certain day.

i. 4, 5 ; v. 5.

II. i.—The Synoptists.

Jesus is a son of David by natural parentage ;

Matt. i. 1—16. Luke iii. 23—38.
Cf. Matt. xiii. 55. Mark vi. 3. Luke ii. 27, 48; iv. 22
John i. 45; vi. 42. Gal. iv. 4 (ἐκ γυναικός, not ἐκ παρθένου
For the current acceptation of the phrase 'born of a woman,'
see Matt. xi. 11).

[1] Cf. Justin, *Apol.* i. 14, 83.

[2] Would not this frequent comparison with angels in i. ii., it has been asked, be altogether superfluous, if the idea of the eternal Second Person of the Trinity had entered into the writer's conception ?

[The two Genealogies of the First and Third Gospels preserve the supposed records of the *"generation"* of Jesus in corrected, though unharmonised, forms. The first is modified by a slight turn in the concluding verse, the second by the insertion of a parenthesis in the opening words.[1] By no other explanation than that of after-adaptation to the altered belief of a later age, is it possible to account for their introduction, or rather for their retention. In their present condition and position they prove nothing. To have been sprung from David by 'legal' succession only, was not, in any fair Messianic sense, to be, "according to the flesh," the son of David at all.[2] On the other hand, there is no Scriptural proof, nor any trustworthy evidence anywhere, of the Davidic descent of Mary. If Joseph and Mary go to "the city of David," it is because *he* is "of the house and family of David" (Luke ii. 4). Moreover, if Acts ii. 30 ("of the fruit of his loins"), xiii. 23 ("of this man's seed"), Rom. i. 3 ("of the seed of David according to the flesh"), 2 Tim. ii. 8 ("of the seed of David"), had been intended, and understood, to refer to the *natural* descent of the mother of Jesus, there

---

[1] For strained explanations of ἐγέννησε and of ὡς ἐνομίζετο, see Wordsworth *ad loc.* and Credner, *Einleitung in das Neue Testament*, p. 68.

[2] "Le Christ devait être plus que l'héritier légal du grand Roi, il devait être matériellement de son sang, aussi bien que du sang d'Abraham. Je ne crois pas qu'il soit possible de révoquer cela en doute."—Père Didon, *Jésus Christ*, Paris, 1891, p. 844. This is an important admission from the conservative side.

would have been no necessity for the weaker argument of two imperfect and irreconcilable attempts to trace the line of descent by *legal* connection through Joseph, the reputed father.—Those who admit that both genealogies profess to give the Davidic descent of Joseph, (apart from the difficulty of the parentage of Shealtiel), in order to reconcile 'Heli' of the second with 'Jacob' of the first, are driven to two violent assumptions, (1) that there was a levirate marriage (Deut. xxv. 6), (2) that the two 'brothers' who had the same wife in succession were not brothers, but half-brothers. See, further, Appendix II. p. 166.]

Not by conception, or birth, but in the moment of baptism, the Holy Spirit descends upon him and he becomes Son of God. A voice from heaven marks the instant of the new birth ;[1]

Matt. iii. 16, 17. Mark i. 10, 11. Luke iii. 22. Cf. 1 John v. 6.

He is still, however, the chosen 'Servant' of Jehovah, and therefore the Divine Sonship expresses rather an ethical than a metaphysical relation ;

Matt. xii. 18. Cf. Matt. ix. 8. Luke, i. 35 ; iii. 38 ; xxiv. 19.

[1] Justin in more than one place identifies the voice from heaven with the words of the Second Psalm : "Thou art my son ; *This day* have I begotten thee." (See Anger's *Synopsis*, p. 22). For the too definite second clause, later revisers of the Gospel Narrative have substituted the colourless words, "in whom I am well pleased." It is singular that S. Paul, on the other hand, in Rom. i. 4 dates the 'determination' of the divine Sonship from the Resurrection, whilst the writer of the Epistle to the Hebrews connects it with the Ascension ; (i. 4., v. 5.)

He ' becomes' full of wisdom ;
Luke ii. 40, 52.

He is liable to temptation and to occasional shadows of ignorance, indecision, dejection, and despair;[1]
Matt. iv. 1—11. Mark xii. 13; xiii. 32. Luke iv. 13.
Matt. xxvi. 38, 39 ; xxvii. 46.
Cf. John vii. 8, 10 ; xii. 27 ; xiii. 21 ; xviii. 7, 34.

He is a ' Prophet' ($\dot{a}v\dot{\eta}\rho \ \pi\rho o\phi\dot{\eta}\tau\eta s$) before God ;
Luke xxiv. 19.

From the Father he receives power and authority, but within certain limits. That which he reveals has been ' delivered' unto him ;
Matt. ix. 8 ; xii. 28 ; xxviii. 18 ; xi. 27.

The Father alone knows and controls the destinies of men : He alone is absolutely and supremely good ;
Matt. xiii. 32; xx. 23. Mark x. 18, 40. Luke xviii. 19.

Jesus, under various titles, is acknowledged to be the Messiah, but the thought of his pre-existence, apparently, has not yet presented itself.[2] For references, see pp. 22—24.

So far we have traced in the First Three Gospels the ground-work of the earliest Christian belief as to the

---

[1] There is no hint or suggestion in the Gospels, or indeed in the New Testament generally, of the Two Natures and Two Wills in One Person which reconciled for theologians of the fifth century the opposed notions of the deity and the humanity of Christ.

[2] It is worthy of notice that the First and Third Synoptists who support the idea of the Miraculous Birth have no idea of the Pre-existence of Christ, whilst the writer of the Fourth Gospel and S. Paul insist on the Pre-existence, but know nothing of any preternatural conception.

being and office of Christ, gathered in from oral
tradition and embedded in the written record. But
fragments of legendary invention, of pious comment,
of ardent forecast, show themselves here and there in
the mass of historic fact. The son of " Joseph," or of
" the carpenter," in one place, becomes the Virgin-born
in another. The descent of the Holy Spirit dates, not
from the day of baptism, but from the moment of
conception ; spiritual affiliation becomes preternatural
generation ; and the anointing of Messiah is lost in the
greater mystery of the overshadowing of Messiah's
mother. The title Son of God reaches a higher than
ethical or theocratic sense (Luke i. 35). He who in
full manhood stood unknown amongst the crowd
(John i. 26) is greeted at his birth by the hosts of
heaven, is adored in his cradle by the lowly and the wise
(Matt. ii. 11 ; Luke ii. 14, 16). All things are delivered
unto him of his Father, and only by the Father is he
known (Matt. xi. 27 ; Luke x. 22). He is transformed
on a holier mount with a brighter transfiguration than
that of Moses, and a flash of more than human glory
dazzles for a moment human eyes (Matt. xvii. 1, 2).
There will be a fuller revelation of his majesty when he
comes on the clouds of heaven and gathers the elect by
his angels from one end of heaven to the other (Matt.
xxiv. 30, 31 ; Luke xxi. 27). He is ' lord '[1] of the

---

[1] In many passages in the Synoptists Jesus is addressed, or
speaks of himself, as Lord (Κύριος). It is clear from Acts
ii. 36 (cf. Ps. cx. 1) that the title could have carried no special

sabbath (Mark ii. 28; Luke vi. 5); he is 'greater'[2] than the temple (Matt. xii. 6); all authority has been given unto him in heaven and on earth (Matt. xxviii. 18); and with his parting words he places his own name between the names of the Father and of the Holy Ghost (Matt. xxviii. 19).

But all these embellishments, pretensions and predictions, extravagant as they are, are still very far from the level of later dogmatic assertion. They embody the musings, inferences and yearnings of a generation of believers too far from the plain facts to be strictly faithful to them, and yet too near altogether to neglect them. Possible modes of pre-existence, distinctions in the Godhead, hypostatic unions, moral dualisms—these are not the subjects which engross the unlettered converts who collected and preserved the reported deeds and utterances of Christ, and we look in vain in their records for deep questionings and subtle solutions. Variations and expansions of current accounts are received, indeed, without scrutiny, and are arranged without harmony. But even speculation has its stages,

significance until after the Resurrection. Its meaning, therefore, in these passages is that which it bears in such places as Matt. xviii. 25, xxi. 30, 40, xxiv. 45, xxvii. 63, &c. The suggestion of any other sense would involve an anachronism. In 1 Cor. vi. 14, viii. 6, the terms 'God' and 'Lord' are contrasted; cf. Ephes. i. 17, Jas. i. 1, 1 Pet. i. 3, Jude 4, 25. See, further, Simcox, *The Writers of the New Testament*, p. 12.

[2] Another reading, μεῖζον, "a greater thing," might possibly denote the 'Gospel.'

and is subject to a law of development, and the time had not yet come for propounding hard problems. In short, there is not a word in the Synoptic Gospels which serves to establish any set doctrine of the deity of Christ. The concluding words of the First Gospel which seem at first sight to hover on the margin of a definition are, as we have seen (Appendix II), a sacramental formula of comparatively late date and are still far removed from the metaphysical, Trinitarian formula into which they were afterwards pressed. And, if the inclusion of the Son in xxviii. 19 is an assertion of deity, what are we to say of the distinction in xii. 32? Would this distinction have been endurable, even to those who were only approaching the belief that, "In this Trinity none is afore, or after other: none is greater, or less than another; But the whole three Persons are co-eternal together: and co-equal?" Cf. John v. 23.

ii.—THE ACTS OF THE APOSTLES.

In the Acts of the Apostles Jesus is :—

A man 'approved,' 'ordained,' 'anointed' by God; of the seed of Abraham; a son of David, *" of the fruit of his loins;"* son of man;

ii. 22; xiii. 38; x. 38; xvii. 31. (Cf. John viii. 40. 1 Tim. ii. 5.)
iii. 25; ii. 30; xiii. 23; vii. 56.

A 'Servant' of God (cf. 1 Pet. ii. 22—25. Matt.

viii. 17 ; xii. 18) ; the ' Righteous One;' the ' Holy and Righteous One ;' a ' Prophet ' like unto Moses.[1]

iii. 13, 26; iv. 27, 30. Cf. iv. 25 ; vii. 52; xxii. 14; iii. 14; ii. 27; iii. 22. Cf. Deut. xviii. 15.

By God he is made :—

A ' Messenger ' to His people ; ' Lord and Christ '[2] (κυρίου for θεοῦ should probably be read in xx. 28); a ' Prince ' and a ' Saviour ;'

x. 36; ii. 36 ; x. 36, 38; iii. 20, (cf. 18) ; iv.27 ; iii. 15; v. 31.

It is by the operation of God that he heals the oppressed, that he is ' raised ' from the dead; by His right hand he is ' exalted ' to heaven, and ' ordained ' Judge of quick and dead ;

x. 38 ; ii. 24, 32 ; iii. 15, 26 ; iv. 10 ; x. 40; ii. 34; iii. 21; v. 31; x. 42.

From God he receives the gifts which he pours upon his church ; at His side he stands, honoured, but distinct ;

ii. 33; vii. 55.

His name is called upon (in prayer) ;[3]

ix. 14, 21 ; xxii. 16; cf. vii. 59 ; 1 Cor. i. 2.

---

[1] " From among your brethren " is a clause which Peter would hardly have quoted if he had known of any pre-existence and miraculous birth.

[2] With τὸν προκεχειρισμένον used of the ' appointment ' of Christ in iii. 20, compare the use of the same word in xx. 14, xxvi. 16. It is easy to see how the idea of pre-determination would quickly become confused with that of pre-existence. Cf. 1 Pet. i. 20.

[3] If this be the meaning of ἐπικαλεῖσθαι, and not rather ' appeal' to a judge, or to a witness, as in Acts xxv. 11, 12, 21, 25 ; xxvi. 32 ; xxviii. 19 ; 2 Cor. i. 23.

He is the ' Son of God,' but the title is considered as synonymous with that of the ' Christ.'

ix. 20, (cf. 22) ; viii. 37 (found in some ancient authorities).

The whole conception is summed up in a single sentence when his chief apostle is made to say of him :—" God anointed him with the Holy Ghost and with power : who went about doing good, and healing all that were oppressed of the devil ; for God was with him."

x. 38.

III. i.—REVELATION.

In this Book Jesus is :—

The ' Root ' and the ' Offspring ' of David ;

v. 5; xxii. 16.

The ' Lion ' of the tribe of Judah ;

v. 5.

The faithful ' Witness ; '

i. 5.

The bright, the morning ' Star ; '

xxii. 16.

' King of Kings,' and ' Lord of Lords ; '

xvii. 14 ; xix. 16.

A ' Lamb ' standing, as though it had been slain, between the throne and the four living creatures ;

v. 6; vii. 17.

The ' Word of God.'

xix. 13.

R

In the last three chapters he ascends in dignity of being and of place. He is :—

The 'Alpha and the Omega;'[1] the 'First and the Last;' the 'Beginning and the End;'

xxii. 13. Cf. i. 17.

The throne of God is also the throne of the Lamb.

xxii. 1, 3.

Like the Angel of Jehovah in the Old Testament, as the minister and representative of God, he is in his operations and titles as God Himself, almost identified with Him. But that the titles are appellative only, and not descriptive of nature, and that the operations are powers delegated and derived, is clear from the following passages, in which the exalted and glorified Jesus is carefully distinguished from the Supreme Being:[2]—

The revelation which he shews unto his servants is 'given' him by God;

i. 1. (Cf. John vii. 16; xiv. 10; xvii. 7, 8.)

As a source of blessing to the churches he is distinct from Jehovah, between Whom and himself stand the Seven Spirits;

i. 4.

---

[1] This title is used of the Lord God in i. 8, and ought to be omitted in i. 11.

[2] For the broad and lax use in Holy Scripture of the term 'God,' and for the transfer to inferior beings of the Sacred Name, see, Gen. xxxi. 29. Exod. iv. 16; vii. 1; xxiii. 21. Isaiah vii. 14; xliii. 6, 7. Jerem. xxiii. 6; xxxiii. 16. Ezek. xlviii. 35. Micah v. 3. In the light of these passages the "Mighty God" of Isaiah, ix. 6, becomes clear.

(?) He is the 'beginning' of the *creation* of God;
(But see the note on πρωτότοκος, p. 227); 'a man child' caught up unto God;

iii. 14. (Cf. Col. i. 15); xii. 5.

The name that he will write upon him that overcometh, is his own '*new*' name;

iii. 12.

Those whom he 'purchased' with his blood, he purchased unto *God;*

v. 9.

To the angel of the church of Sardis he says, "I have found no works of thine fulfilled before '*my*' God;" and to the church in Philadelphia, "He that overcometh, I will make him a pillar in the temple of '*my*' God;"

iii. 2; iii. 12. Cf. John xx. 17.

In the same way the Kingdom is the kingdom of our LORD and of '*His*' Christ, or the kingdom of our God and the authority of '*His*' Christ;

xi. 15; xi. 10.

Finally, God is "his God and Father."

i. 6.[1]

---

[1] It has been contended that, if the writer had meant "*His* God," he would have repeated the possessive genitive, αὐτοῦ, according to his usual practice—*e.g.*, vi. 11, ix. 21. But there seems to be no reason why the co-ordinate titles should not be rendered here as in Rom. xv. 6; 2 Cor. i. 3, xi. 31; Eph. i. 3; 1 Pet. i. 3, and the Revisers have evidently been of that opinion.

ii.—The Epistles of S. John.[1]

Jesus Christ is :—

> I. i. 3 ; iii. 23 ; v. 6.

From the beginning ;[2]

> I. i. 1 ; ii. 13, 14.

Only begotten ;

> I. iv. 9.

Sent into the world ;

> I. iv. 9, 14.

Incarnate ;[3]

> I. ii. 22 ; II. 7.

The ' Name ;'

> III. 7.

The ' Holy One ;'

> I. ii. 20.

Sinless ;

> I. iii. 3, 5, 7.   Cf. ii. 1.

Light ;

> I. ii. 8.

[1] The relative dates of the First Epistle and of the Fourth Gospel are uncertain. The former seems to pre-suppose an acquaintance with at least the leading statements of the latter. Weizsäcker gives priority to the Gospel ; Westcott, on the other hand, seems to think that the latter *in written form* was subsequent to the Epistle.

[2] It is difficult to say where the writer means the initial point to be placed, for in iii. 8, the same phrase, ἀπ' ἀρχῆς, is used of the devil who "sinneth from the beginning." In i. 2, "the word of life" is used with reference to the Gospel, and not to Christ personally. See Westcott, *Epp. of St. John*, pp. 6, 7.

[3] A second Advent is glanced at in I. ii. 28.

Life ;

I. v. 11—13.

Knowledge ;

I. v. 20.

An ' Advocate ' with the Father ;

I. ii. 1.

The ' Christ ; '

I. ii. 22 ; v. 1. II. 7, 9.

The ' Son of God ; '[1]

I. i. 3, 7 ; ii. 22—24 ; iii. 8, 23 ; iv. 9, 14, 15 ; v. 5, 9—14, 20.
II. 3, 9.

But the climax of the argument in the Epistles, as in the Gospel, is that Jesus is the Christ, the Anointed of God. "Whosoever believeth that Jesus is the Christ is begotten of God." Not that he is God, but that he is the Christ of God—this is the sum of the believer's faith, this the distinguishing mark of the children, the ' begotten,' of God.

I. v. 1. (Cf. John xx. 31).

Here also, as in the Gospel, the Father is the ἀληθινὸς θεός, the ' true God.'[2]

I. v. 20. (Cf. John xvii. 3).

[1] This name, notwithstanding the introduction of the term *Logos*, has in the Johannine writings, as in the New Testament generally, only the ethical, theocratic, Messianic sense which it bears in the Old Testament. See John xx. 31. I John v. 1, 5. It is of Messiah, not of the Second Person of the Trinity, that the Evangelist is thinking ; of God's Son, not of God the Son. But see *infr.* 247, Note 2.

[2] Attempts have been made (conspicuously by Dr. Liddon *Bampton Lecture*, p. 358) to identify the υἱὸς of the preceding

iii.—The Fourth Gospel.

In the Synoptists a human being becomes divine; in the Fourth Gospel Divine Being becomes man; 'becomes' flesh, and makes of a human body a temporary (?) abode.[1] For the use of σκήνη and σκηνόω, which do not necessarily imply in themselves temporariness of sojourn, see Rev. vii. 15, xxi. 3.

> i. 14; vi. 62; xvii. 5. (Cf. 1 John iv. 2, 3. 2 John 7).

He is:—

The 'Heavenly Man'; cf. Rom. v. 15. 1 Cor. xv. 21, 45;

> iii. 13; vi. 62.

Pre-existent;

> i. 1, 2, 15; iii. 31; vi. 38, 46; viii. 23, 42, 56, 58; xvi. 28; xvii. 5, 24; cf. xii. 41.

Only begotten;[2]

> i. 14, 18; iii. 16, 18. (Cf. 1 John iv. 9).

clause with the ἀληθινὸς θεός of the closing sentence. If the reader incline to the same view, let him consult Bp. Westcott's frank and exhaustive note *ad loc., The Epistles of St. John,* p. 196, and the able discussion of the passage in Beyschlag, *Christologie,* pp. 149, 150. If further argument be needed, let him compare John xvii. 3.

[1] A little examination will show that the 'ἐρχόμενον ἐν σαρκί' of 2 John 7, is not, as has been supposed, against this view. Baur sees in vii. 10, 15, viii. 59, x. 39, vi. 19—21 indications of a belief on the part of the Writer that the 'tabernacle' of the flesh was in some of its qualities unlike the ordinary human body; but the evidence, strong in itself, is weakened by comparison with other passages, *e.g.,* vii. 1, xii. 54.

[2] Not with reference to any 'eternal generation,' but in the LXX and N.T. sense of μονογενής, *unicus,* unique, one of its kind, 'only.' See Westcott, *Epistles of S. John,* p. 169.

All knowing; (But cf. iv. 1, xi. 34);
i. 49; ii. 25; iv. 17; vi. 64, 70; xi. 4, 14; xiii. 38; xvi. 30.

Sinless;
vii. 18; viii. 29, 46, 55; xiv. 30; xv. 10.

Creative;
i. 3, 9, 10, 11; vi. 44.

Administrative;
iii. 35; v. 22, 27, 30; xiii. 3.

The 'Light' and 'Life' of the world; [i. 4, says Luthardt, need not refer to the pre-existent so much as to the incarnate Word];
i. 4, 5, 9; vi. 35; viii. 12; xi. 25; xiv. 6.

The 'Holy One' of God;
vi. 69.

The 'Word;'
i. 1, 14.

The 'Son of God' (the Christ);[1] cf. Acts ix. 20, 22;
i. 49; iii. 35; ix. 35; xi. 4, 27; xx. 31.

Divine ($\theta\epsilon\acute{o}\varsigma$); and, in a manner,
i. 1, and, perhaps, 18.

'God.'[2]
xiv. 28; xx. 28 (cf. xii. 41; xiv. 10; 2 Cor. v. 19.)

[1] It has been contended (Gess, *Christi Person*, &c., 539) that in the following passages the title 'Son of God' is more than the equivalent of the title 'The Christ'—iii. 16—18, v. 17—26, vi. 40, viii. 36, x. 36, xiv. 13, xvii. 1. All that we can do is to weigh them against the places cited above.

[2] Cf. the similar identification of the 'Angel of Jehovah' with Jehovah in Gen. xxii. 11, 12, Exod. iii. 2, 6, 14.

But he is dependent on the Father and inferior[3] to Him ; by Him he is consecrated and sent into the world ; by Him he is inspired ;

v. 19—32; viii. 40 ; xiv. 28 ; x. 36 ; iii. 34 ; iv. 34 ; v. 23, 24, 38 ; vi. 57 ; xi. 42 ; xiii. 20 ; xvii. 18 ; xx. 21 ; iii. 34 ; i. 32.

In the Father's name he comes, and to Him he prays, not only on earth, but when enthroned in heaven ;

v. 43 ; xii. 27 ; xiv. 16 ; xvii. 1.

He is one with the Father, but it is a moral union—" That they may be one, *even as we* are one ;"

x. 30, 38 ; xiv. 10, 20, 23 ; xvii. 22, 23.

He is also external to God ; $\pi\rho\grave{o}\varsigma\ \tau\grave{o}\nu\ \Theta\epsilon\acute{o}\nu^1$; $\pi\alpha\rho\grave{a}\ \tau\overline{o}\upsilon\ \Theta\epsilon\overline{o}\upsilon$; $\epsilon\grave{\iota}\varsigma\ \tau\grave{o}\nu\ \kappa\acute{o}\lambda\pi o\nu\ \tau o\overline{\upsilon}\ \pi\alpha\tau\rho\acute{o}\varsigma$; $\pi\alpha\rho\grave{a}\ \tau\tilde{\wp}\ \pi\alpha\tau\rho\acute{\iota}$; $\acute{o}\rho\tilde{a}\nu,\ \acute{a}\kappa o\acute{\upsilon}\epsilon\iota\nu,\ \tau\grave{o}\nu\ \pi\alpha\tau\acute{\epsilon}\rho\alpha$; $\acute{a}\pi\grave{o}\ \Theta\epsilon o\overline{\upsilon}$;

i. 1 ; xiii. 3 ; vi. 46 ; i. 18 ; viii. 38 ; xvii. 5. ; vi. 46 ; viii. 40 ; xiii. 3.

The life which he has is a gift, his words and his works are not his own ;

v. 26 ; vi. 57 ; v. 36 ; vii. 16—18 ; viii. 28 ; xiv. 10, 24 ; xvii. 8.

Not only is he 'sanctified' and 'sealed,' 'taught' and 'sent' by God, but he speaks of himself as 'a man' that has told the truth which he '*heard*' from God ;

x. 36 ; vi. 27 ; vii. 28 ; viii. 28, 42, 40 (cf. 26) ; xv. 15 ; v. 27.

He does not separate himself from his people when he says, " We worship that which we know;"

iv. 22 ; cf. 21, 23.

---

[3] In the doctrine of the *Logos* the inferiority of the Word was a necessary condition, in order that connection might be established between God and man.

It is not only to his ' Father,' but to his ' God ' that he ascends;

xx. 17.

The Father he knows and reveals ; he is His Prophet and Witness to His truth ; but the Father alone is " the True God ;" " the Only God."[1]

viii. 55 ; x. 15, 37 ; xiv. 10 ; iv. 44 ; iii. 11, 32 ; xviii. 37 ; xvii. 3, v. 44.

It is clear from the foregoing pages that there are three stages in the development of the Christology of the New Testament :—

i. The earlier portions of the Synoptic Gospels, the Acts of the Apostles, the First Epistle of Peter and the Epistles of James and Jude, exhibiting Judaic Christianity in its simplest and purest form, present Christ as foreknown, but not pre-existent, a man approved, ordained, anointed, raised from the dead, and exalted to heaven, by God.   To these writers the title

---

[1] In x. 34 " the Jews" are represented as saying that they sought to stone Jesus because, being a man, he made himself God.   Here was the place for saying frankly, either, "I am God," or "I am not God, though I am His Son."   The reply which is put into his mouth is evasive and irrelevant.   Compare also the forced connection between *v.* 17 and *v.* 18 in chapter v. Not only is the second verse a most improbable inference from the first, but, in the light of many passages in the Synoptists, it is impossible to believe that a dialogue like this could have taken place at the very beginning of the ministry.   There are other instances in which the writer of the Fourth Gospel seems to play with his subject and to make it his aim, not so much to satisfy as to mystify his readers.

'Son of God' determines, not the nature, but the office, of the Christ. They find in Jesus the fulfilment of ancient prophecy, and they are unaffected by the philosophising, speculative tendencies of Alexandrian and other semi-ethnic thought.

ii. The teaching of the Pauline School affirms the pre-existence of Christ, but the pre-existence is not that of a Second Person in the Godhead, but of a *divine principle* which developed and manifested itself in a human life. This doctrine is set forth in terms which approach very closely to the Johannine doctrine of the *Logos.* Christ is the 'Image,' the 'Form,' the 'Effulgence,' the 'Impress,' through which the invisible, unapproachable God reveals Himself to men.[1] Inasmuch as men also are, in a sense, made in the image and after the likeness of God, Christ is therefore the Ideal Man, the Archetype of all the Sons of God. This teaching knows as little of two 'Natures' in Christ as of two 'Persons' in the Godhead.[2] He was born, like all men, 'according to the flesh,' and 'according to the spirit.' True, his spirit is the 'spirit of holiness,' (Rom. i. 4. 1 Tim. iii. 16), and

---

[1] In ἀπαύγασμα the thought of 'personality' finds no place; and in χαρακτήρ the thought of 'coessentiality' finds no place. Westcott, *Epistle to the Hebrews,* p. 425. This is an important admission.

[2] "It is unscriptural, though the practice is supported by strong patristric authority, to regard the Lord during His historic life as acting now by His human and now by His Divine Nature only."—Westcott.

therefore his flesh is without spot of sin, but the two factors constitute ' The One Man.' He is the glorified Head of Humanity, and, when his work has been fulfilled and the faithful have been conformed to the image of the Son, then he will surrender his office, and God will be all in all.

iii. In the Johannine Writings some of the terms which describe the pre-existent Christ are less concrete than those just mentioned. He is now the Alpha and the Omega, the Name, the Word, and the distinction of being becomes very fine in the θεὸς ἦν ὁ λόγος of the Prologue of the Fourth Gospel ; but the many and various supplementary titles which abound in these books, and the sense of the passages in which they are introduced, make it difficult to believe that the writer was less anxious than other teachers to distinguish the Christ from the '' True and only God.''

Mention may here be made of the *Kenosis*, or self-emptying, theory, by which to perplexed believers the amazing process of Incarnation is softened, and the difficulties of the ''limited human knowledge'' of Christ, the self-limitation by which he '' condescended not to know,'' are explained. The doctrine is based on Phil. ii. 6—9 (cf. 2. Cor. viii. 9), in which place it is said that Jesus '' being (originally) in (the) form of God, counted it not a prize (a thing to be clutched) to be on an equality with God, but ἑαυτὸν ἐκένωσε,'' &c. This is understood to mean that, being God, he divested

himself of the Glory of Deity, the Divine Prerogatives.
Now, in the first place, the force of κενοῦν in the
Pauline Epistles—Rom. iv. 14; 1 Cor. i. 17; ix. 15;
2 Cor. ix. 3—is not to strip, to divest, but to "make
void." This is exactly rendered in the Authorised Version by "made himself of no reputation," now changed
in the Revised Version to "emptied himself." The
whole passage need not mean more than that Christ,
though in form divine, did not, as he fairly might,
grasp at godlike honour,[1] but made himself void; so to
speak, disparaged himself; taking less than his due.
If reference be intended to any temporary laying aside
of the glories and prerogatives of Deity, which in that
case might rightfully be resumed, how are the *exaltation*,
and *bestowal* of a new "name," by God in *v.* 9 to be
explained? Ὑπάρχων, it is true, implies prior existence,
but existence prior to a definite act is not necessarily
eternal. There is nothing to prevent the inclusion of
ἐκένωσε in the idea of voluntary humiliation on earth,
more fully expressed in the 8th verse.

But, apart from the consideration of this particular
text, the whole tenor of New Testament argument is
against this theory of pre-historic self-divestment. Far
from representing Christ as spontaneously stripping
himself of his majesty and power, the Writers describe
him rather as a passive instrument in the hands of his

---

[1] To allow that τὸ εἶναι ἴσα θεῷ may possibly mean "equality
with God" is not at all to allow that it means identity with
God.

Father. By the Father he is ' consecrated,' ' sent,' and
' brought' into the world, ' made' a little lower than the
angels, ' named' a high priest, ' determined' to be Son,
' appointed ' heir of all things, ' ordained' a judge,
' raised' from the dead, ' exalted' to heaven, ' counted
worthy' of and ' crowned' with glory, ' endowed' with
greater powers and new titles. From the Father he
receives ' a body,' moral ' perfection,' ' revelation,'
' gifts,' ' dominion,' ' glory ;' by Him he is ' taught'
and ' sealed.'

INDEX.

I.—OLD TESTAMENT.

II.—APOCRYPHA.

III.—NEW TESTAMENT.

S